Reserve Component Unit Stability

Effects on Deployability and Training

Thomas F. Lippiatt, J. Michael Polich

Prepared for the Office of the Secretary of Defense

NATIONAL DEFENSE RESEARCH INSTITUTE

The research described in this report was prepared for the Office of the Secretary of Defense (OSD). The research was conducted in the RAND National Defense Research Institute, a federally funded research and development center sponsored by OSD, the Joint Staff, the Unified Combatant Commands, the Department of the Navy, the Marine Corps, the defense agencies, and the defense Intelligence Community under Contract W74V8H-06-C-0002.

Library of Congress Cataloging-in-Publication Data

Lippiatt, T.
    Reserve component unit stability : effects on deployability and training / Thomas F. Lippiatt, J. Michael Polich.
        p. cm.
    Includes bibliographical references.
    ISBN 978-0-8330-4962-9 (pbk. : alk. paper)
    1. United States. Army Reserve—Unit cohesion. 2. United States. Army Reserve—Personnel management. 3. United States. Army Reserve—Operational readiness. 4. United States. Army Reserve—Mobilization. I. Polich, J. Michael. II. Title.

    UA42.L54 2010
    355.3'7—dc22

                                                                                    2010026524

The RAND Corporation is a nonprofit research organization providing objective analysis and effective solutions that address the challenges facing the public and private sectors around the world. RAND's publications do not necessarily reflect the opinions of its research clients and sponsors.

RAND® is a registered trademark.

Published 2010 by the RAND Corporation
1776 Main Street, P.O. Box 2138, Santa Monica, CA 90407-2138
1200 South Hayes Street, Arlington, VA 22202-5050
4570 Fifth Avenue, Suite 600, Pittsburgh, PA 15213-2665
RAND URL: http://www.rand.org/
To order RAND documents or to obtain additional information, contact
Distribution Services: Telephone: (310) 451-7002;
Fax: (310) 451-6915; Email: order@rand.org

Preface

This monograph describes results of a research project on unit personnel stability in the Reserve Components (RCs) of the U.S. Army.[1] As the pace of RC unit mobilization has quickened in the past several years, personnel instability in units has emerged as a potential problem, particularly in units that are preparing to deploy to a theater of operations. Such instability—for example, personnel leaving the unit and being replaced by others before deployment—could produce a number of undesirable effects. However, the U.S. Department of Defense (DoD) had little systematic data available to measure instability in deploying units or the effects that may flow from it.

The purpose of the project was to quantify the rate of personnel movement, to investigate the causes of that instability, to identify effects on training, and to examine possible policy changes that DoD might institute to manage instability and its effects.

This document is the final report of a research project titled "Unit Stability and Its Effect on Deployability and Training Readiness," sponsored by the Assistant Secretary of Defense for Reserve Affairs. The research was conducted within the Forces and Resources Policy Center of the RAND National Defense Research Institute, a federally funded research and development center sponsored by the Office of the Secretary of Defense, the Joint Staff, the Unified Combatant Commands, the Navy, the Marine Corps, the defense agencies, and the defense Intelligence Community.

For more information on RAND's Forces and Resources Policy Center, contact the Director, James R. Hosek. He can be reached by email at James_Hosek@rand.org; by phone at 310-393-0411, extension 7183; or by mail at the RAND Corporation, 1776 Main Street, P.O. Box 2138, Santa Monica, California 90407-2138. More information about RAND is available at www.rand.org.

---

[1] *Stability*, as used in this monograph, refers to the degree to which a unit's membership remains constant over time. In a stable unit, relatively few people leave or enter the unit during a given period of time. In a less stable unit, by contrast, members frequently leave the unit and must be replaced by others.

Contents

Figures

Tables

Summary

Personnel stability is highly valued by all military forces, particularly in combat units and other formations that deploy to a theater of operations. The Army in particular aims to maximize unit stability—that is, the degree to which a unit's membership remains constant over time. Yet, RC units typically experience a surge of personnel turbulence as they approach mobilization and deployment. Some members leave the unit, and new personnel are cross-leveled into the unit to reach its target for deploying strength. This inflow of personnel undercuts the effectiveness of training because new arrivals miss training events that have occurred before they join. As a result, units must repeat some training, making pre-mobilization preparation less efficient and impeding the training of successively higher echelons.

How widespread is this problem, what causes it, and what might be done about it? RAND research was undertaken to address those questions, focusing on these issues:

- stability levels of personnel in deploying RC units
- how long units are stabilized before deployment
- the major factors that generate instability
- the potential effect of instability on unit training
- policy options that could help manage the situation.

The research was based on longitudinal data assembled from DoD monthly records for all personnel who were in any Army component from 1996 through 2008. We used that database to trace the preparation and deployment of three classes of units in the Army National Guard and U.S. Army Reserve: infantry battalions, military police (MP) companies, and truck companies.[1] The resulting analysis included 153 RC unit deployments, representing more than 40,000 authorized positions. The selected classes of units span the major types of Army units (combat, combat support, and combat service support), and they are generally representative of elements that deployed as whole units.

Instability Is Widespread

As a unit approaches mobilization and deployment, one might expect that it would maintain a stable cohort of members to permit efficient and sequential training of the myriad tasks that must be mastered before deployment. However, the data showed that *in*stability, rather than

---

[1] The three classes of units generated five different types of units for analysis: National Guard infantry units, MP units in both the Guard and Reserve, and truck units in both the Guard and Reserve. The Reserve contains very little infantry.

stability, is the rule. Across five types of RC units that we studied in detail, covering deployments from 2003 through 2008, RC units experienced substantial instability in their run-up to deployment. Of all the soldiers who actually deployed with those units, 40 to 50 percent were "new arrivals" who had been in the unit less than one year.[2]

This picture of instability is no fluke. We found that it is widespread across all types of deploying units, even those that initially enjoyed high fill rates (e.g., more than 90 percent of authorized positions filled one year before mobilization). Similar levels of instability also exist in active units; in some cases, active units are less stable than their RC counterparts. In addition, pre-deployment instability affected all grade levels—not just junior enlisted personnel but also noncommissioned officers (NCOs) and officers. In fact, officer instability was the highest of all grade groups, owing to the tendency for officers to be transferred out of a deploying unit into another unit—often "cross-leveled" into a unit that deployed even earlier than their source unit.

Causes and Effects of Instability

What accounts for this instability? We identified several factors—primarily, personnel losses during the year before deployment and the presence of numerous "nondeployers" (personnel who did not deploy with their unit). These two factors prompted a large influx of new people before mobilization. In fact, so many people were moved that, by the deployment date ("D-day"), the units were manned at rates of 115 to 125 percent of authorized positions.

A major role was played by personnel losses—soldiers leaving the unit because of moving to another unit or leaving the service entirely. Across the five unit types studied, between 25 and 40 percent of personnel who were assigned to the unit 12 months before mobilization had left the unit during the subsequent year. However, these loss rates may be more benign than the numbers might suggest. First of all, these loss rates appear "normal." The fraction of people leaving the service has remained almost constant since the year 2000, and it was no higher during the year before deployment than it was during the preceding year. So, losses did not rise appreciably as deployment approached. Second, many of the losses *from the unit* were not losses *from the Army*. Particularly among officers and NCOs, a majority of those leaving the unit had transferred to another unit; often, those same soldiers deployed with their new unit, sometimes even before their source unit deployed.

The other major factor was nondeployers. About 30 percent of soldiers in the RC units at D-day did not deploy. Many different conditions contribute to this picture. Some did not deploy with the unit but then moved to another unit. Some remained at home station and later deployed to their unit in theater, and some were activated and remained at home station, evidently as part of a rear detachment. Some had recent prior activations and so were probably exempted from another deployment for a period of time. Some were new recruits who had not yet completed initial training. And some were not even activated.

Among the various groups of losses and nondeployers, it seems likely that, in some cases, they represent an Army accommodation to the service member's personal circumstances or hardship; the Army may have preferred to defer a soldier's deployment or permit a move to

---

[2] Current plans call for units to be notified of an upcoming deployment at least one year beforehand, and they generally execute pre-mobilization preparation and training over that year.

another unit than to lose the person to the Army altogether. In other cases, instability arises from deliberate Army actions (e.g., to fill high-priority deploying units) or from the effects of conditions that are normal features of the reserves (such as the presence of untrained new recruits, who cannot be deployed until they finish training).

Finally, there are many different groups with different conditions that contribute to the overall picture of instability. Most of the groups represent just a small fraction of the problem, and many would be difficult to affect by policy. When we analyzed the probable effects of different possible policy interventions, it was clear that, even with multiple policy changes and reasonable degrees of success, a large gap would remain between the unit's targeted deploying strength and the number of its members who would be "stable"—i.e., people who have been in the unit for one year or more upon deployment. We concluded, therefore, that RC units are not likely to reduce instability to the vanishing point. The RC will have to live with a substantial amount of instability in the run-up to mobilization and deployment.

How does this instability affect training as the unit prepares for deployment? The key observation is that the rapid buildup of personnel begins at about six months before mobilization. Yet, units have been conducting important training events over a longer period of time, often 12 months or more. When that training is done early, the new arrivals miss key events, and, therefore, the unit must arrange repeat training for them. To examine that process, we plotted the buildup curves of people who eventually deployed, to show the inflow of personnel during the last 12 months before deployment, compared with the major training events in unit training plans. In some cases, training on significant subjects—such as combat training center exercises, combat lifesaver training, urban warfare techniques, and dealing with improvised explosive devices—were conducted early enough that 30 to 50 percent of the deployers would have missed them. That pattern was common across all major types of units studied.

In fact, we saw several unit training plans that included specific "makeup" training precisely for that purpose. That is bound to affect the efficiency of both individual and unit training; the unit's leadership must manage training sessions and events for the new arrivals, expend training support resources to cover them, and perhaps defer follow-on training (e.g., for more-complex tasks or collective training).

Options for Managing Instability

What policy options does that leave for DoD? For the near term, we outlined four alternatives that recognize the likelihood of continuing personnel instability:

- *Stretch training over many months (current policy).* The Army could simply accept existing rates of instability, the need to repeat some training for new arrivals in the unit, the concomitant bill for training resources, and limits on the speed with which the unit can be readied.
- *Cluster training just before mobilization.* If the most-intensive training were compressed into the last five months or so before mobilization and finished up during a short post-mobilization training period, that training would reach 75 to 80 percent of the soldiers who deploy with the unit. The inefficiencies of doing training earlier would be avoided, and most soldiers would be together during key training events. However, such a course imposes a greater burden on soldiers, families, and employers, concentrated in one time

period. It could also result in lower participation rates in pre-mobilization events if their time demands are seen as burdensome.

- *Increase duration of mobilization.* This option would move much of the intensive training into the post-mobilization period, thus relieving the pressure on pre-mobilization and ensuring that soldiers are together for training. An obvious drawback is that it would require relaxation of limits imposed in recently announced DoD policy, and it would keep soldiers away from their homes and civilian jobs for a longer period of time.
- *Reduce boots-on-the-ground (BOG) time.* A fourth option would be to concentrate training after mobilization as above but retain the 12-month time limit on the duration of mobilization. Consequently, it would reduce BOG time in theater. While gaining the same training advantages as the third option, it would require a faster unit turnover rate in theater and, therefore, more units to cover a given period of operations.

For the longer term, the monograph also considers more-aggressive initiatives with which DoD might experiment. Particularly if cyclical deployments continue, the chain of command will surely seek methods of enhancing stability and training efficiency. Such initiatives might aim to foster better unit-level retention, control interunit moves, lower vacancies through intensified recruiting, accelerate initial training, and enhance medical and dental screening or treatment. In addition, DoD might try other initiatives to enhance training efficiency, such as more centralized training, greater use of mobile training teams, and distributing individual training to personnel who will move into a deploying unit just before mobilization. Each of the above types of initiatives could require substantial investments and would need to be evaluated over the long term. If successful, they might reduce instability, make training more efficient, or both. However, at present, there are no data that allow us to judge the prospects for success or the magnitude of possible savings. Therefore, it would be wise to test such initiatives on a small scale to acquire credible evidence of their actual effects and costs.

Abbreviations

AC	Active Component
AIT	Advanced Individual Training
ARNG	Army National Guard
AT	Annual Training
BDE	brigade
BOG	boots on the ground
CONUS	continental United States
CTC	combat training center
D-day	deployment date
DMDC	Defense Manpower Data Center
DoD	U.S. Department of Defense
ECP	entry control-point operations
Ex CTC	externally supported combat training center event
FRG	Family Readiness Group
IDT	Inactive Duty Training
IED	improvised explosive device
M-day	mobilization date
MEDVAC	medical evacuation
MOS	military occupational specialty
MP	military police
NCO	noncommissioned officer
PMI	preventive maintenance and inspections
PTAE	Provisional Training Assistance Element

QRF	quick-reaction force
RC	Reserve Component
ROTC	Reserve Officer Training Corps
RTC	Reserve Training Center
SA	situational awareness
SRC	standard requirements code
SRP	soldier readiness program
TDA	Table of Distribution and Allowances
TOE	Table of Organization and Equipment
TSIRT	theater-specific individual readiness training
TTHS	Trainees, Transients, Holdees, and Students
USAR	U.S. Army Reserve
WEX	Work Experience File
WFX	warfighter exercise

CHAPTER ONE

Introduction

Personnel stability is highly valued by all military forces, particularly in combat units and other formations that deploy to a theater of operations. Yet, Army units, including those in the Reserve Components (RCs), commonly experience high levels of *instability*—that is, the departure of some unit members and their replacement by others. In fact, basic features of RC units inevitably generate a considerable amount of personnel instability, which is accentuated as they prepare for mobilization and deployment. This monograph examines the rate of instability, its primary causes, potential effects on training, and policy options for dealing with instability and its effects in deploying units.

Personnel instability has posed a more visible problem in recent years as the Army has mobilized large numbers of RC units for operational missions. RC units aim to accomplish much of their preparation *before* mobilization; that helps to keep the post-mobilization period as short as possible, thereby maximizing the unit's time in theater and minimizing the time that soldiers are away from their homes, families, and civilian jobs. However, personnel instability works at cross-purposes to quick and efficient training—and, as a result, it may limit the scope of training that can be accomplished. Therefore, we wanted to understand the extent of pre-mobilization instability, the main factors that produce it, and the ways in which it affects the efficiency of pre-mobilization training.

Why Stability Is Important

What is personnel stability? The basic concept refers to the degree to which a unit's membership remains constant over time. In a stable unit, turnover rates will be low and, hence, many members will have long tenure in the unit.[1]

Why is stability an important concern? All commanders prefer personnel stability in their units, particularly as they prepare to go to war. One reason is the difficulty of training a unit that is undergoing personnel turbulence—some soldiers leaving and being replaced by others who are "new arrivals."[2] If the unit is not stable, it must repeat some elements of training for

---

[1] In fact, we will measure stability by aggregating the tenure levels of individuals in the unit. The more members with long tenure, the more stable the unit. Thus, a stable unit is one in which many individuals have been assigned to the unit for a long time—say, more than one year. In some of our empirical analysis, we use that criterion as an operational definition of *stability*.

[2] In military environments, the terms *personnel turbulence* and *turnover* are often treated as synonyms for instability. Although these other terms sometimes carry slightly different connotations, in this monograph, we use them to refer to the same basic phenomenon.

newcomers, thus consuming more resources and time. Furthermore, the resulting inefficiency may impede training of successively higher echelons (even teams or crews), or it may prevent training on more-difficult tasks that require simpler skills as a foundation.[3]

Personnel instability is especially relevant for reserve forces because they have less time to train than active units. In peacetime, a typical RC unit has about 39 days per year available for training: Inactive Duty Training (IDT), usually a two-day set of "drill periods" done one weekend per month at home station, and a 15-day Annual Training (AT) period, often involving exercises at a large military installation. In contrast, active units have the entire year available. So, if a reserve unit is hit by personnel turbulence, it has less time to recover and fewer resources to fall back on. Moreover, a considerable part of an RC unit's available time is consumed by administrative tasks, setting up and preparing for training events, managing equipment, and traveling to and from training sites. These "overhead" costs further reduce the amount of time available for actual training in an RC unit.

In wartime—or preparation for a deployment—these issues are more critical. The unit must ensure that all soldiers have proper personnel and pay records, legal documents, immunizations, personal equipment, basic skills, and a host of other things. Soldiers must undergo training required by the overseas combatant command and training on theater-specific tasks. They may need to receive and become familiar with special equipment not available at home station. And, because these actions take place in a compressed time schedule leading to a fixed arrival date in theater, personnel turbulence poses a distraction that can slow down training and make it less effective.

Special Challenges for Deploying Reserve Component Units

RC units face several conditions that exacerbate personnel instability. First, they experience a substantial rate of personnel turbulence in peacetime. Previous RAND analyses have found that a typical unit loses 20 to 30 percent of its personnel each year.[4] Active units also have substantial turbulence rates, but, as noted earlier, they have more time to recover and usually benefit from being stationed at a large Army installation that makes personnel administration and training more efficient from the unit's point of view.

Beyond that "normal" level of instability, reserve units must expect further personnel turbulence as they prepare for operations, even if they have maintained a relatively stable cohort up to that point. One reason is that most RC units begin with less-than-ideal personnel fill; many units have fill rates (number of persons assigned divided by the number authorized) under 90 percent, sometimes much lower. Unfilled positions leave vacancies that must be filled before the unit deploys, so the filling process creates turbulence all by itself.

---

[3]   As an example, consider an important team task called "clearing a room," as sketched by a former battalion commander (Peterson, 2008, p. 15). This task is a demanding group effort requiring coordination and teamwork. It must be repeated at several levels of complexity to achieve full proficiency. If one team member departs, the team is deemed "unqualified" and must repeat the sequence of exercises to develop both individual and group skills.

[4]   This level of personnel turbulence consistently appears in studies conducted at many points in time. See, for example, Buddin and Grissmer (1994); Kirby, Grissmer, and Schlegel (1993); and Sortor et al. (1994). More recently, our own tabulations based on Defense Manpower Data Center (DMDC) data from 2001 through 2007 show year-to-year unit-level loss rates ranging from about 20 to 30 percent.

In addition, all reserve forces contain a sizable group of new recruits—usually between 5 and 10 percent—who are "untrained." Those people are new entrants who have signed up for service, attend drills, and receive pay but who have not yet completed initial entry training (basic training and skill training for their military occupation).[5] Untrained soldiers cannot be deployed, by law. Their presence in the unit means that they must be replaced before deployment—creating more personnel instability—or sent to school on a priority basis to complete their training. That is a problem unique to the RC; active units generally receive their most junior members from the central personnel system, which assigns them to units only after they have completed initial training.

These problems are often portrayed as if they arise primarily from the arrival of new nonprior-service recruits. However, turbulence also affects the unit leadership, including both noncommissioned officers (NCOs) and officers. Although ideally the leadership would remain stable and provide continuity for training and unit management, in fact, leaders may leave the unit for a wide variety of reasons. For example, they may transfer to another unit to obtain a promotion or broader experience, as part of regular professional development. They may go away from the unit temporarily for formal military professional education at an Army school. They may move their household to another geographic area for civilian employment or family reasons, thus necessitating transfer to a different RC unit. And, not uncommonly during the recent period of intense RC utilization, some leaders may be transferred ("cross-leveled") by the Army to fill another unit that is about to deploy.

The result is that an RC unit preparing for mobilization and deployment may experience a surge of personnel turbulence. As the preparation for mobilization proceeds, many new personnel are cross-leveled into the unit to reach its target for deploying strength. This inflow of personnel creates a period of heightened activity and turbulence, coming at a time when the unit and its members are already under pressure to complete pre-deployment requirements, hone their skills, and prepare for operations. The result is what we would term an unstable deploying unit: one in which many soldiers have very short tenure in the unit.

Effects of the Operational Reserve Policy

All of these problems are well known and have persisted for many decades. However, they were brought into sharper focus by the advent of rotational deployments and the U.S. Department of Defense (DoD) doctrine of the "operational reserve" (DoD, 2008). Today, RC units are being regularly and repeatedly mobilized and deployed, in contrast to earlier periods, when reserve forces were used much less frequently and were generally mobilized only for a major

---

[5]   Normally, a new entrant attends basic training at an Army installation and then acquires an occupational skill in a course of Advanced Individual Training (AIT) managed by the Army school for his or her branch specialty (e.g., infantry, armor, military police, transportation). The soldier is awarded a military occupational specialty (MOS) upon graduation from AIT. Only such graduates are available for deployment to an overseas theater. Many new RC recruits require a considerable period of time to attend both types of school, and they experience lags due to course scheduling constraints, their personal schedules, and other factors. The Army has attempted to cope with this problem by establishing a special Trainees, Transients, Holdees, and Students (TTHS) account for such persons, but, thus far, it has not eliminated the problem in the RC.

contingency or national emergency.[6] The continued pace of mobilizations since 2001 has both stressed the system and revealed the extent of personnel instability during a unit's ramp-up to deployment.

A recent change in DoD policy has accentuated the need for quick unit training and personnel stability. In early 2007, the Secretary of Defense announced new guidelines for reserve deployments, including a provision that limits the length of a unit's mobilization to 12 months (Gates, 2007). Within that 12-month period, the unit must complete any last-minute tasks, including post-mobilization training that reserve units have always required.[7] At the same time, the Army wants the unit to proceed through the post-mobilization preparation as quickly as possible to allow the maximum amount of time in theater with "boots on the ground" (BOG time).

Those circumstances place a premium on conducting pre-mobilization training earlier in the process, generally at IDT assemblies, AT, or special training events that may last several days to a few weeks. In fact, many units preparing for deployment have scheduled more than one AT period or other special event (sometimes lasting two to three weeks) during the last year before mobilization. However, the effectiveness and efficiency of those early preparations are potentially undermined by personnel instability, which works at cross-purposes to efficient and timely training. The primary motivation for this study was to determine how much instability exists in deploying units and how it affects training in an environment in which the Army is seeking to conduct pre-mobilization training quickly and efficiently.[8]

Stability in a Broader Context

Our interest in stability centers on its role in pre-mobilization training. However, there are other perspectives, some heatedly debated within the defense community, that ascribe additional pros and cons to stability. Although these are not the subject of this monograph and our data cannot address them, we outline them here because ultimate decisions about personnel policy may need to consider these divergent perspectives.

---

[6] DoD figures show that the number of reservists called up between 2001 and 2008 was about 650,000, compared with 267,000 in the first Persian Gulf War and 3,000 in the Vietnam War (Office of the Assistant Secretary of Defense for Reserve Affairs, 2008, p. 8).

[7] As an example, some collective training events can be conducted only at an installation with appropriate ranges and maneuver areas, and with specialized facilities and assessment methods that cannot be easily replicated at RC unit home stations. That is only one example; many other actions must be taken in the post-mobilization period, ranging from routine personnel administration to equipment fill to medical examinations and procedures.

[8] This study was limited to Army units, for two reasons. First, Army units account for the lion's share of deployed personnel. According to data we obtained from the Defense Manpower Data Center (DMDC), Army personnel who deployed to Iraq and Afghanistan between 2003 and 2008 represented 74 percent of all military personnel deployed to those operations. Among all deployed reservists, Army RC personnel accounted for about 80 percent.

In addition, the 12-month mobilization limitation imposed by the Secretary of Defense affects the Army much more than other services. The Marine Corps and Air Force deploy their personnel for shorter periods of time, usually on the order of six to seven months; they can mobilize RC personnel, train for an extended period of time, and still execute a planned deployment within the DoD guidelines.

Pros: Presumptive Advantages of Stability

Military culture articulates a pronounced preference for stability in units. U.S. military journals, testimony, and speeches by the leadership are replete with references to the need for stability and the positive results to be expected from it (e.g., White, 2002; Harvey and Schoomaker, 2005; Brinkerhoff, 2004). Indeed, military pronouncements often imply that turbulence is always bad—that stability is good and that the Army needs more of it.

This sentiment stems in part from the advantages of training a unit that is stable rather than unstable. However, there are at least two other considerations often advanced to support the contention that personnel turbulence is too high and more stability is needed.

Continuity of Leadership. One consideration, which we have heard articulated by officers who oversee training of reserve units, concerns continuity of leadership. If leadership changes, the unit suffers weakened ties between officers/sergeants and unit members. Perhaps more importantly, if leadership turns over in an RC unit, the new leaders have not necessarily gone through the entire process of preparation and training with their unit. As a result, they may not have observed the unit's performance in its sequential training exercises, and they may not fully understand the unit members' experience, capabilities, and strengths and weaknesses. In addition, the new leaders may not feel the sense of "ownership" that long-standing leaders would possess.

Unit Performance. A much more prominent belief is the expectation that more-stable units will perform better in combat. That belief is strong and widely held; it is so intuitive and so common that it approaches being an article of faith in military circles (Griffith, 2007; Peterson, 2008). It is based on an underlying theory that stable units achieve greater cohesion among unit members and that the higher level of cohesion fosters improved unit performance.

However, research has found only spotty and inconclusive evidence on the actual empirical relationships among stability, cohesion, and performance. The theory that ties those concepts together stemmed originally from interviews of prisoners of war and American soldiers during World War II (Shils and Janowitz, 1948; Stouffer et al., 1949); those studies pointed to cohesion (e.g., close personal relationships among a "primary group," such as a squad or group of buddies) as a key factor that kept a unit fighting even in the face of stress or overwhelming opposing force. Although those studies received much attention in the aftermath of World War II, systematic research since then has produced a more complex and inconclusive set of results. Later researchers distinguished "task cohesion" (common commitment to a shared goal) from "social cohesion" (feelings of attraction or camaraderie), but only task cohesion has been found to be associated with operational performance, and, even there, the evidence is ambiguous (MacCoun, 1993; MacCoun, Kier, and Belkin, 2006; Mullen and Cooper, 1994; Peterson, 2008). A common interpretation is that social cohesion keeps units from disintegrating even under stressful or hopeless conditions, but probably does not make them fight *better*. Task cohesion may enhance quality of performance, though the relationship is controversial (Winkler, 2008). Nevertheless, proponents of cohesion continue to assert its primacy, prompting contentious debate between the theory's adherents and critics.[9] This has produced a decidedly murky picture of cohesion and its possible linkage to performance.

What's more, there is virtually no evidence to link personnel stability *directly* to operational performance. Such a link is hard to prove, since operational performance is notoriously

---

[9]   See, for example, the exchange in a leading journal pertaining to a study of cohesion in the Iraq war (Wong, 2006; Wong et al., 2003; MacCoun, Kier, and Belkin, 2006; Kolditz, 2006; Griffith, 2007).

difficult to measure. Several researchers have searched for such a link empirically, in the context of tank crew gunnery and exercises of maneuver units and command groups at the Army's combat training centers. But they have not found a significant relationship between unit performance and personnel stability (Keesling, 1995; Peterson, 2008). Furthermore, even if there were a relationship, to inform policy, one would want to know more than the simple existence of a correlation: For example, how much does performance improve as a function of stability levels and the length of time the unit has been stable? Unfortunately, the research literature is silent on such questions.

We conclude that stability *might* be related to performance under some conditions, but the connection is tenuous at best. In contrast, we can directly observe the effects of stability on training, and training is the immediate concern of this study. Moreover, as we will see, most deploying units are not able to attain high levels of stability, despite Army policies and measures to promote it. Therefore, the entire question may be moot. Accordingly, this monograph examines the relationship of stability to pre-mobilization training but does not claim to treat the possible effects on combat performance.

Cons: Some Potential Downsides of Stability

Most observers tend to see personnel stability as an unalloyed benefit. However, it is possible that stability also has some downsides. Some authors (Peterson, 2008; Staw, 1980; Winkler, 2008) suggest that some level of personnel movement may be good, even necessary for the health and vitality of units.

Army Flexibility. For example, the Army needs some flexibility in how it mans units. Some unit personnel may be needed elsewhere for other duties, such as to work on higher-echelon staffs or to fill vacancies in other units that are deploying immediately. From the larger viewpoint of developing the officer and NCO corps, it may also be desirable to assign people to schools or other professional development assignments, even if their current unit is on track to deploy. These competing goals may explain why previous Army initiatives to stabilize soldiers in operational units have repeatedly failed or been abandoned (Brinkerhoff, 2004; Towell, 2004).

Skills. Another reason for reassigning soldiers may lie in their skill set. A unit may need to replace personnel who lack appropriate qualifications or skills that will be needed in an imminent deployment. The chain of command may need to replace technicians who have not achieved qualification or certification, personnel who lack skills for a newly defined mission, those who are underperforming, and people who have medical conditions that may limit their performance in theater. It can even be argued that units need a certain amount of "new blood" to bring fresh ideas or a leavening of experience gained in other assignments (Peterson, 2008).

Accommodation. In addition, the Army may prefer to accommodate soldiers who need to defer a deployment because of civilian job change, college enrollment, personal hardship, temporary medical condition, pregnancy, or other reason. In some cases, accommodating such soldiers can allow the Army to retain a person who might otherwise leave the Army altogether.

We do not have detailed data on these potential positive and negative factors. Our interest lies in measuring existing rates of instability and inferring their effects on training in the pre-mobilization period. Stability may have some of the broader effects that we have just outlined, but those effects lie outside the scope of this monograph.

Purpose and Content of This Monograph

This monograph was prepared to document research into the extent and effects of personnel instability. When our research began, there was little empirical analysis to establish some key facts, such as

- stability levels of personnel in deploying units
- how long units are stabilized before deployment
- the major factors that generate instability
- the potential effect of instability on unit training and continuity of leadership.

This monograph is organized into seven additional sections that deal in turn with our database and methodology; stability levels as observed in deployments between 2003 and 2008; variations across unit types, grades, and components; personnel dynamics that create instability, including unit losses, gains, and nondeployable personnel; effects of instability on training; and policy options that DoD could consider in light of these findings.

In the course of the monograph, we present the following key findings and arguments:

- RC units that deployed between 2003 and 2008 experienced substantial personnel instability in their run-up to deployment. Nearly half of the soldiers who deployed had less than one year's tenure in their unit.
- Instability is widespread across all types of units and grade levels—including unit leadership.
- Instability arises from several different factors—especially losses and nondeployers—prompting a large influx of gains before mobilization.
- Losses and nondeployers arise from numerous diverse causes, many of which are difficult to control.
- Despite much pre-mobilization turbulence, RC units did achieve a relatively stable cohort of deployers after mobilization.
- Instability affects training effectiveness and efficiency, especially given the 12-month limitation on mobilization.
- Instability undercuts training that is extended over a year or more before mobilization; as a result, efficiency considerations argue for scheduling most training at a point close to mobilization. This raises several options for policy that point in different directions, posing trade-offs for DoD to weigh and decide.

Chapter Two describes the unique database on which this research was based and our methodology for employing it. Chapters Three through Seven then present the details of analysis and findings that amplify the above points. After a conclusion in Chapter Eight, an appendix supplies additional data.

Data and Approach

Integrated Longitudinal Database

The analysis in the current monograph is based on a unique database available for this project. The database contained monthly individual records for all personnel who were in any Army component during the period from January 1996 through December 2008. To track the history and movements of soldiers in deploying units, we collaborated with DMDC to create an integrated historical database merged by the individual person's identifier, including the following information:

- *individual personnel history:* grade, MOS, entry date, initial military training, unit assignment, and other characteristics from DMDC's Work Experience File (WEX)
- *activation and deployment:* month of activation and return from active duty and month of deployment to theater and redeployment to the United States, from DMDC's Defense Mobilization and Deployment database[1]
- *pay:* records of actual pay, allowances, bonuses, and other monetary compensation (including hostile-fire pay), from the defense Reserve and Active Duty Pay files.

The resulting merged file permitted us to conduct longitudinal analysis of individuals and units, tracking sequences of events over time, both during "normal operations" and during the run-up to mobilization and deployment. It allowed us to discern key time-phased events, such as reservists going on active duty and deployment of individuals, whole units, or large parts of units.

The database also permitted analysis of groups of people within a unit to determine the unit's behavior as well as that of individuals. For example, we could see small numbers of individuals in a given unit being activated and deployed over a period of several months (e.g., as an advance party), then a subsequent surge of activations and deployments as the main body of troops deployed, and, later, successive returns of small and large numbers of troops by month. It also permitted us to examine cohorts of individuals, such as people who were assigned to the unit one year before mobilization, and to track them over time to determine whether they remained in the unit until deployment and whether each particular individual actually deployed with the unit.

---

[1] The database covers all deployments to all operations that carried hostile-fire pay, starting in the year 2001. We supplemented that information with records of hostile-fire pay for preceding years.

Scope of Unit Types and Deployments

Unit Types Selected for Analysis

The analysis included data from the Army National Guard (ARNG), the U.S. Army Reserve (USAR), and the Active Component (AC). In this document, we report primarily on information from the two RCs, but, in a few cases, we have included some comparison data for the AC.

Within each component, we focused on three specific classes of units:[2]

- *infantry battalions*[3] within separate brigades (ARNG)
- *military police (MP) companies*, "combat support" type (ARNG and USAR)
- *truck companies*, "medium cargo" type (ARNG and USAR).

Within these types of units, we obtained data on all deploying units, provided that they met the following criteria:

- deployed between *January 2003 and June 2008*[4]
- deployed essentially as a *full unit*—that is, deployed strength represented at least 75 percent of the unit's authorized positions.

Table 2.1 shows the designations and personnel authorizations of these units, from the Army's Master Force files. The three classes of units were selected to span the range of RC units along several dimensions. First, they represent the three main categories of Army Table of Organization and Equipment (TOE) units: combat, combat support, and combat service support.[5] They cover many of the sizable units that deployed frequently and essentially as whole units. They include a large number of people; for example, there are nearly 20,000 positions in the ARNG infantry units, and several thousand in the MP and truck companies within each RC. Finally, each individual unit is large enough to yield reasonably stable statistics; the battalions contain nearly 700 positions each, while the companies range from about 160 to 180 positions each.

Table 2.1 also shows abbreviations we will use as shorthand for the five types of reserve units. In Army data systems, the ARNG is designated as component 2 and the USAR as component 3. Accordingly, we designate ARNG infantry battalions as IN2, ARNG MP companies as MP2, USAR MP companies as MP3, and so forth, as shown in the table.

In all, the selection criteria yielded 153 RC unit deployments for analysis. Virtually all of the RC units had no prior deployments since 2001, although some had prior continental

---

[2] Each class of units is defined by one or more specific standard requirements codes (SRCs), which can be linked to the unit's required personnel, equipment, and other assets. For example, one SRC defines "combat support" MP units, as compared with other units that handle prisoners or conduct criminal investigations. These designations and requirements vary slightly over time; we took that into account in analyzing each unit for each year.

[3] The ARNG contains almost all of the Army's RC infantry battalions. The USAR has one such battalion, but it is atypical and we omitted it.

[4] Our period of observation continued until the end of 2008, but we used an earlier cutoff date that allowed us to track the behavior of individuals for at least six months after deployment.

[5] Units described as TOE are generally configured to deploy and fight or conduct operational missions in the field. They are contrasted with TDA (Table of Distribution and Allowances) units, which typically perform training, support, or administrative functions and do not deploy.

Table 2.1
Types of Units Selected for Analysis

Unit Type	Component	Abbreviation	Number of Units	Average Number Authorized	Total Authorized Personnel
Infantry battalion	ARNG	IN2	29	674	19,546
MP company	ARNG	MP2	41	178	7,298
	USAR	MP3	15	177	2,655
Truck company	ARNG	TK2	32	170	5,440
	USAR	TK3	36	161	5,796

NOTE: In addition, the database included the same three types of AC units: 77 infantry battalions, 89 MP companies, and 21 truck companies.

United States (CONUS) mobilizations. So, in effect, the RC units were undertaking their first full mobilization and deployment since 2001.

Generalizability

When selecting a subset of units such as this one, a question may arise: Is this subset representative of the larger "universe" to which it refers? From these types of units, can we generalize to a wider set? In this monograph, our interest focuses on the stability of preexisting units that were called to mobilize and deploy as unitary entities—that is, effectively as "whole" units. The research question is this: When deployed, do these units contain a stable complement of personnel who have been together for an appreciable period of time?

The deployment of whole units is the traditional focus of stability concerns, often expressed as maintaining unit integrity. That phenomenon can be examined, however, only by analyzing units that actually did deploy as relatively complete entities. So, what kinds of units did deploy in that way? Our review of unit and individual deployment data from 2003 through 2008 showed that the three branches listed in Table 2.1—infantry, MP, and truck units—represented a large portion of all units that deployed at 75 percent of authorized level or higher.[6] Only a couple of other unit types (engineers and quartermaster branches) had an appreciable number of qualifying units, and their unit counts were much smaller, which would yield a small sample size. Therefore, we selected the infantry, MP, and truck units with confidence that they account for the bulk of units in the universe to which we wish to generalize.

It should be noted, however, that this universe of units that deploy as full formations is a subset of the total Army deployment picture. It does not necessarily represent smaller elements, such as partial units, specially formed detachments, nonstandard formations, or call-ups of individuals to fill specific theater requirements.

---

[6]   On average, these units deployed at a strength equal to about 85 percent of their authorized level during the single month that we selected to represent the onset of the unit's deployment. If one counted other unit personnel who deployed slightly earlier or later, the figure would be about 90 percent.

Unit Level

One other caveat applies to these data. We measured stability at the level of "unit identification code," which meant battalion for the infantry and company for the MP and truck units.[7] The data do not permit us to reliably distinguish smaller groups, such as platoon, squads, or teams. As a result, the data could mask greater turbulence at the lower echelons. For example, a soldier could move from one platoon or squad to another within the same company, but that would not appear as a move in our data.

Approach to the Analysis

In the chapters that follow, we determine the profiles of units to describe their personnel stability and composition over time as they prepare to deploy. In particular, we want to quantify key patterns of personnel movement:

- *losses:* personnel leaving the unit
- *gains:* personnel moving into the unit
- *nondeployers:* unit personnel who do not deploy.

We then use those data to examine three important patterns of personnel movement surrounding the deployment preparation process. In sequence, the chapters will provide the following:

- a *retrospective* look at soldiers in unit at the time of deployment—building a picture of unit stability before deployment
- a *prospective* look at soldiers who leave the unit during the year before mobilization
- a *prospective* look at soldiers who are in the unit at the time of deployment but who do not deploy.

Each of those patterns is revealing as a way of quantifying rates of personnel instability in deploying units and explaining the factors that create that instability.

---

[7] Technically, we used the first four characters of the official six-character unit identification code. The latter two characters are designed to represent subelements of a battalion or company, but, in practice, the personnel systems do not reliably track people in those elements.

CHAPTER THREE

Stability Levels in Deploying Units

From the point of view of deploying units, *stability* means having a complement of soldiers who have been assigned to the unit for a considerable period of time. That means long enough to have trained together and have participated in pre-mobilization preparation events, which are often scheduled over a period of ten to 12 months before mobilization. Therefore, we adopted, as a working definition of *stability*, a measure of 12 months in the unit.

Figure 3.1 displays the result of applying this definition to ARNG infantry battalions at the time they deployed. Among those battalions, in the aggregate, 44 percent of the soldiers were "new arrivals," meaning that they had arrived at the unit during the 12 months preceding the unit's month of deployment. The remaining 56 percent were "stable": members who had been in the unit for more than 12 months.[1]

While that level of stability may seem low to some observers, Figure 3.2 shows that it is not unique to infantry units. This figure shows the same information as in Figure 3.1 for all five types of units that we studied in detail, using the unit type abbreviations that were defined

Figure 3.1
Stability Rates in Deploying Army National Guard Infantry Battalions

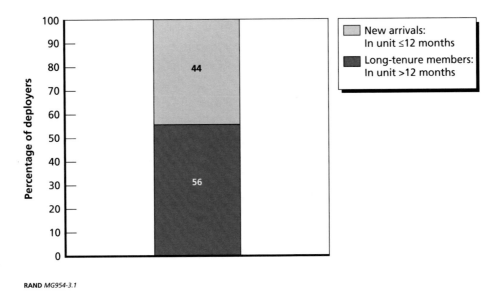

RAND *MG954-3.1*

---

[1] This is a summarized version of much more-detailed data. Each unit member has a tenure, his or her length of time in the unit. The more people with long tenures, the more stable the unit. The appendix shows details of the distribution of tenure, by month, for all five types of units.

Figure 3.2
Stability Rates in Five Types of Deploying Units

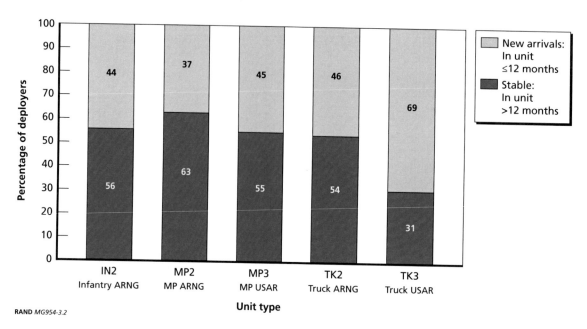

RAND *MG954-3.2*

in Table 2.1. In fact, among most types of units that we examined, a figure of 40 to 50 percent new arrivals is common. In the USAR truck companies, the figure is considerably higher: 69 percent of all deployers were new arrivals in the unit. As we will discuss in more detail below, this high rate of instability for USAR trucks continued over time and reflects extensive cross-leveling among units of that type.[2]

Does this pattern of turbulence affect the leadership? Some might expect that most of the instability would occur among junior enlisted personnel, whereas the NCO and officer leadership might be more stable. However, that is not the case, as illustrated by Figure 3.3. In fact, personnel turbulence is widespread across all grades of soldiers.

It is true that NCOs are more stable than the other grade groups. However, even among NCOs, in four of the five types of units, only about 55 to 70 percent of NCOs had been assigned to the unit for a year or longer at the time of unit deployment. That means that about one-third to one-half of the NCOs were new to the unit.

The picture is more unstable for other grade groups. Junior enlisted personnel are slightly less likely to be stable than NCOs. And officers are the *least likely* to be stable. Even in the infantry battalions, where personnel stability is often said to be particularly prized because of the need for extensive collective training, about half of the deploying officers were new arrivals in the unit during the past year.

Nor is this level of instability confined to the reserve forces only. Figure 3.4 shows stability rates for the deploying AC units compared with the ARNG and USAR. This shows that AC infantry battalions are just as unstable as National Guard battalions. AC military police and truck companies are even less stable than their RC counterparts. Among MP units, only

---

[2]   Another type of instability, turnover during the unit's service in theater, could theoretically be relevant to unit integrity while it is performing a mission. However, we found that in-theater manning rates were generally quite stable, changing by only a few percentage points during the deployment and mainly occurring near the end of the deployment.

Figure 3.3
Stability Rates by Grade and Unit Type

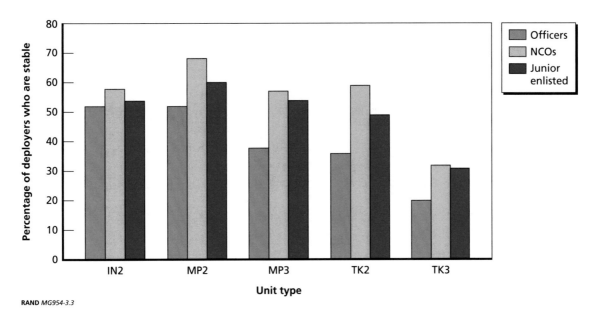

RAND *MG954-3.3*

Figure 3.4
Stability Rates for Active and Reserve Component Deploying Units

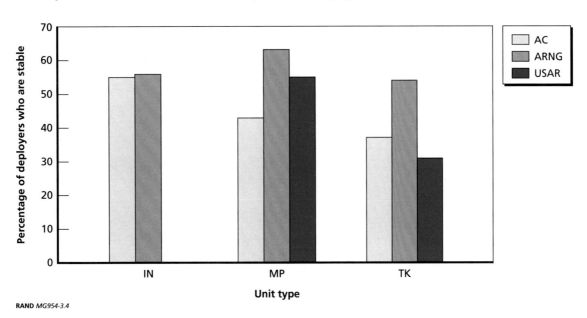

RAND *MG954-3.4*

42 percent of personnel in AC units were stable, compared with between 55 and 65 percent of RC units.

Factors Creating Instability

The level of instability, its widespread distribution, and its persistence over time (from 2003 through 2008 in these units) suggest that it is no fluke. And it seems remarkable given the high value placed on personnel stability and cohesion in military circles and Army policy. So we asked this question: What factors create instability in deploying units?

By tracing the history of individuals and their patterns of movement over time, we observed three primary factors that create personnel turbulence in deploying units:

- *fill rates:* vacancies created by lack of personnel to fill required positions
- *losses:* departure of soldiers from the unit
- *nondeployers:* personnel who remain assigned to the unit but do not deploy with it.

Figure 3.5 illustrates these factors and the magnitude of key parameters by which they can be measured. It traces personnel over the one-year period before the main body of the unit deployed. In the analysis that follows, the beginning of this period is designated as $D - 12$ (12 months before deployment), and the end of the period is designated as D (the month when most unit members who deployed departed for the theater of operations).[3] The figure portrays

Figure 3.5
Factors Creating Instability in Deploying Units: Infantry Battalions

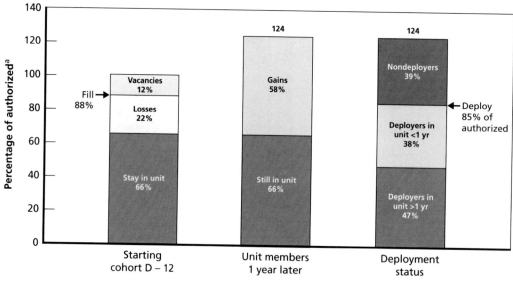

^aBased on number of TOE authorized; number required in theater may vary.

RAND MG954-3.5

---

[3]   To define D, the initial unit deployment month, we first determined the largest number of personnel from that unit who were deployed during any given month—the "peak" number. Then we scanned the preceding months and declared the initial deployment month as the first month when 95 percent of the peak number were deployed. This generally captured the point at which a surge of people went to theater, normally a much larger group than in any preceding month.

effects exerted by the three factors, as they unfold over that period for the case of ARNG infantry battalions.

Vacancies

To begin with, the infantry battalions had vacancies amounting to 12 percent of their authorized positions, on average. Thus, as shown in the leftmost bar, the fill rate was only 88 percent. To the extent that required positions are vacant, the Army must find other personnel to move into the unit ("cross-leveling"). Lack of complete personnel fill was one factor that generated personnel turbulence as the unit prepared to deploy. However, as is evident from the figure, it was by no means the predominant factor for infantry units. (In other types of units, as we will see, low fill rates exerted considerable effect on turbulence.)

Losses

Over the course of the ensuing year, naturally, the units experienced some outflow of personnel; they are "losses" from the unit's point of view. In the case of infantry battalions, between one-fifth and one-fourth of the soldiers who were present in the unit at D – 12 had left the unit by D-day. This group, which amounted to 22 percent of authorizations, is illustrated by the middle portion of the left bar in the figure. After those losses, the unit had only 66 percent of its authorized strength that had remained in the unit for one year or more at the time of deployment.

It is important to bear in mind that these losses represent people who are departing *from the unit* but not necessarily from the Army. Some of the soldiers who left the unit were simply transferring to other Army units, so their "loss" would affect the source unit but not the overall manpower posture of the Army. We will examine these distinctions among types of losses in detail in the next chapter.

Together, the large number of losses and vacancies left the unit with a considerable shortfall of personnel. We do not have precise unit-by-unit data on the size of the unit requested by the theater, but, for elements that were deploying essentially as whole units, we would expect the target fill rate to be at least 85 to 90 percent of authorized strength.[4] In this case, the unit had only 66 percent of authorized positions filled by stable soldiers. That situation induced a large influx of new arrivals over the year before deployment. For the average infantry unit, the Army added a large number of new personnel—the "gains" shown in the upper portion of the center bar. The number of new arrivals was equal to 58 percent of the authorized strength. These were added to the 66 percent who had already been in the unit for more than one year. In total, then, by D-day, the average infantry battalion was manned at a level well above its nominal authorized strength: 124 percent of authorized.

---

[4] Figure 3.5 shows that these units, on average, deployed 85 percent of their authorized strength during the month in which the main body of the unit left. However, a small number of people joined the unit in theater thereafter. So the total strength of the unit in theater was generally at 90 percent or higher.

Note that the figure displays the number of deployers as a fraction of TOE-authorized positions, not the number requested by the combatant command. Often, the theater commander requested formations whose composition varied from the normal makeup of a unit—sometimes only a partial unit. If the theater requested formations whose size was smaller than authorized strength, then the number deploying could easily be 100 percent of the request.

Nondeployers

At first, this temporary overmanning situation may seem anomalous. One might think that the unit was positioned to deploy at a very high level of strength, with a considerable margin to spare. However, we found that a substantial fraction of the personnel assigned to the unit did not, in the end, deploy with the unit.

The right bar in the figure shows the actual distribution of unit personnel when the unit deployed. Among all of the individuals assigned to the unit, almost one-third did not deploy (39 percent of authorized, compared with 124 percent total unit membership). That left the unit with a number of deployers equal to 85 percent of its authorized strength, as shown by the arrow at the right.

How stable was the resulting group of deploying soldiers? As shown by the two lower portions of the right bar in the figure, people who had been in the unit for one year or more represented 47 percent of authorized, and the new arrivals represented 38 percent. Thus, there were almost as many newcomers in the unit as long-tenure members.[5]

These patterns are generally replicated across the other types of units studied. They raise important questions such as these, for both losses and nondeployers:

- What kinds of people account for losses and nondeployers?
- What happens to those people after they leave the unit or fail to deploy? Where do they go, and what does that imply about the reasons for their behavior?

The following two chapters address these questions, first for losses and then for nondeployers.

---

[5] These figures are consistent with the results displayed earlier in Figure 3.1. That is, stable-unit members represented about 55 percent of all deployers (47/85), and new arrivals represented the remaining 45 percent.

CHAPTER FOUR

Losses from Units Approaching Deployment

Because personnel losses play such a large role in instability, we wanted to understand better the conditions and phenomena that cause people to leave a unit that is approaching mobilization and deployment. To do so, we created longitudinal records of individuals in specific units over one-year windows, as exemplified in Figure 4.1.

The most important period, the subject of our investigation, is the one-year period at the right of the figure: the *year before mobilization*, what we call the M-1 year. It begins 12 months before mobilization and ends when the unit is officially mobilized (mobilization day, or M-day).[1] We tracked all individual soldiers who had been in the unit at the point 12 months earlier and ascertained their status over the next year, ending at M-day. We call this group the pre-mobilization cohort. The analysis focused on the pre-mobilization period because we wanted to explore the feasibility of intensive training before mobilization. In addition, we expected minimal turbulence after mobilization, and that expectation was borne out in the empirical data.

Figure 4.1
Time Periods for Assessing Three Cohorts of Unit Personnel

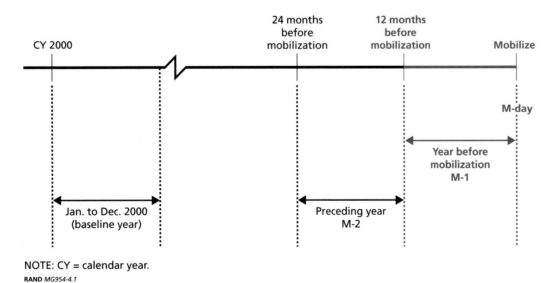

NOTE: CY = calendar year.
RAND *MG954-4.1*

---

[1]   Mobilization (on what is conventionally described as M-day) typically occurs two to four months before deployment. Since recent policy changes added to pre-mobilization training requirements, this chapter focuses on personnel losses in the period before M-day. Units are relatively stable between mobilization and deployment.

We also tracked two similar one-year cohorts from preceding periods, to compare the pre-mobilization cohort with similar groups of soldiers in earlier periods of relatively normal operations:

- *M – 24 months cohort:* This period began at 24 months before mobilization (M – 24 months) and ended at 12 months before mobilization. The personnel were from the same units as the pre-mobilization cohort. We reasoned that, during this year, the unit had not been alerted and members of the unit were not necessarily anticipating an impending deployment. So their tendency to stay or move out of the unit would, generally speaking, represent the behavior of soldiers in a "normal" (nonmobilizing) unit during a period when the Army was involved in extensive overseas operations.
- *year 2000 cohort:* This period began in January 2000 and ended in December 2000. Again, the personnel were from the same units as the pre-mobilization cohort. This period, of course, was before the commencement of operations in Iraq and Afghanistan and well before the doctrine of an "operational reserve" was articulated.

Figure 4.2 exhibits loss rates during the year before mobilization. For example, the left-most bar shows the history of all personnel who were in National Guard infantry battalions that deployed during the period 2003–2008. Of those personnel who were assigned to the unit at the point 12 months before mobilization, 26 percent had left the unit by the mobilization point. As can readily be seen from the figure, such a loss rate was not unusually high. In fact, the loss rates among our five types of units ranged from 26 percent to 39 percent.

It should be understood that these are aggregate loss rates, summed across all units within each unit type. The loss rates for some individual units, of course, are considerably lower, while others are higher. For example, among the 29 infantry battalions, the mean loss rate was 26 percent, as shown in Figure 4.2. However, one-fourth of the battalions (the lower quartile) had loss rates at 19 percent or below, while another one-fourth (the upper quartile) had rates at

Figure 4.2
Unit Loss Rates for Five Types of Units, During the 12 Months Before Mobilization

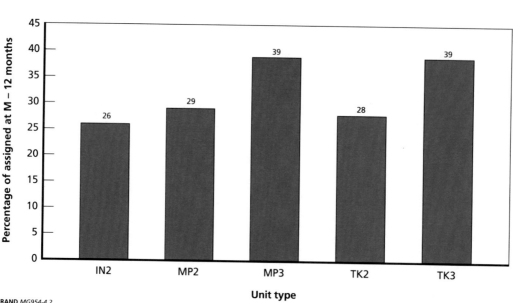

29 percent or above. The appendix shows summary statistics on the distribution of loss and fill rates across individual units. It shows that fairly high loss rates are not uncommon; for example, the upper quartile among ARNG MP and truck units stands at about 35 percent, while, among USAR MP and truck units, it stands at 50 percent or higher. That means, for example, that one-fourth of all USAR MP and truck units lost 50 percent or more of their people over a one-year period. We do not have insights to explain the reasons for variations across individual units, but the data underscore the fact that many reserve units must live with substantial loss rates even during the period when they are approaching mobilization.

To probe some of the reasons for those losses, we subdivided the personnel in the pre-mobilization cohort, as illustrated in Figure 4.3 for infantry battalions. The figure begins with all those soldiers who were assigned to the unit at M – 12 months (the leftmost column in the figure), here portrayed as 100 percent of assigned.[2] In the next column, we show the status of those soldiers one year later, at the time the unit mobilized. At the mobilization point, 74 percent of the original cohort was still assigned to the unit, while 26 percent had left the unit.

The third column further subdivides the stayers and leavers. The upper portion of the figure shows what happened to the 74 percent who had remained in the unit. As of M-day, 54 percent of the original cohort had deployed with the unit; another 20 percent remained assigned to the unit but did not deploy with the main body of the unit. The lower pair of boxes in that column shows what happened to the 26 percent of the original cohort who had left the

Figure 4.3
What Happened to Soldiers Who Were in the Unit 12 Months Before Mobilization

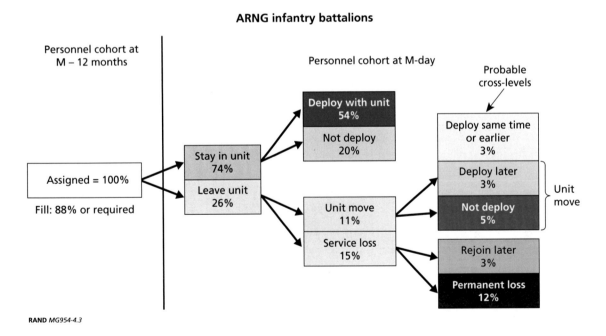

ARNG infantry battalions

RAND MG954-4.3

---

2   In fact, as we have seen before, this number was not sufficient to fill the unit completely; those assigned amounted to only 88 percent of the unit's official requirement.

unit: 15 percent had left the service altogether, and the other 11 percent had moved to another Army unit.[3]

Finally, at the upper right, we see three subsets of the 11 percent who moved to another unit:

- Three percent moved to another unit and deployed at the same time or earlier than the unit to which the soldier had been originally assigned. On average, these individuals deployed seven months before their original unit deployed. We subsequently refer to these people as *probable cross-levels*, reflecting our inference that the Army deliberately moved them (or they volunteered to be moved) into a unit that was even closer to deployment and probably urgently needed additional personnel.
- Three percent moved to another unit that eventually deployed, but their deployments occurred later than the deployment of their source unit—on average, 15 months later.
- Five percent moved to a unit that did not deploy during our period of observation.[4]

Interpreting these last two groups is somewhat ambiguous. The individuals may have moved to another unit to defer their eventual mobilization or to avoid it altogether. The Army may have been willing to accommodate those individuals, particularly if the local commanders perceived that the alternative might be to lose the person altogether from the Army. On the other hand, some of these moves could be due to geographic movement of the soldier's household (for example, due to civilian employment or to be nearer to family) or to attain promotion in another unit that had a vacancy at the requisite grade.

At the lower right of Figure 4.3, we see details of the 15 percent who left the service. Among that group,

- 12 percent were permanent service losses
- 3 percent were people who left the service but rejoined it later—on average, 13 months after they had departed.

Next, we examine further details about the history of various people in the five boxes at the right, first for service losses and then for unit moves.[5]

---

[3] Almost all of the unit moves were to another unit in the same component. There were very few moves across components—say, from the ARNG to the AC or to the USAR.

[4] The period of observation lasted from 2003 through 2008, and most of the deploying units deployed in the first few years of that period. So, for most individuals in this sample, there was a period of several years—say, from 2005 through 2008—when they could have been deployed within the window of possible observations.

[5] The statistics displayed here are aggregated across all units in a specific unit type; for example, the figure of 15 percent service losses represents the aggregated number of losses in infantry battalions as a fraction of all personnel assigned to infantry battalions. There is some variation across individual battalions, but, in general, the picture is one in which most units experience a substantial rate of losses and unit moves. Details of the individual unit distributions are summarized in the appendix, which shows the median, quartiles, and upper and lower tenth percentiles of those distributions.

Service Losses

For the service losses, we examined the three different time periods specified at the beginning of this chapter: the pre-mobilization year, the M-2 year (second year before mobilization), and calendar 2000. Figure 4.4 shows that service-loss rates have been remarkably stable, even going back to the year 2000. In all three cohorts, permanent loss rates hover around 12 percent. And, in most unit types, another 3 percent or so leave the service but later rejoin.

Two important conclusions can be drawn from these data. First, service-loss rates in these types of units have not risen appreciably since 2000. That is, despite the unprecedented rate of RC call-ups and tempo of operations, the Army's RCs in these unit types are losing no larger fraction of people than they lost during the comparatively low-tempo period preceding operations in Iraq and Afghanistan.[6] Second, there is no apparent tendency for soldiers to leave the unit—or "bail out"—as the unit approaches a deployment. Some might expect that soldiers would leave the service as they anticipate their unit being deployed. If such an effect were real, we would expect to see loss rates increase between the M-2 year (when units have generally not been notified of an upcoming deployment) and the M-1 year (when the unit is generally in the midst of preparation for an impending deployment).

Figure 4.4
Service Loss Rates over Three Time Periods

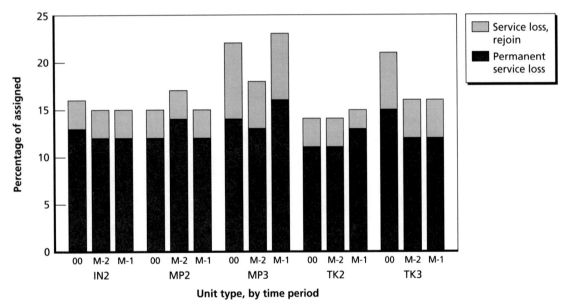

NOTE: 00 = calendar year 2000. M-2 = year from M – 24 months to M – 12 months. M-1 = year from M – 12 months to M-day.
RAND *MG954-4.4*

---

6   Recall, though, that retention bonuses and other inducements to retain people have risen precipitously since the earlier period, according to the pay data. Without such incentives, the picture might be considerably different.

Unit Moves

A different picture emerges for unit losses that represent interunit transfers, as shown in Figure 4.5. This figure exhibits the three groups of unit moves that were portrayed earlier in the example of infantry battalions, but, this time, we calculated the loss rates for each type of unit and for each of the three time periods.

This figure shows that unit moves were common, even in the base year 2000. Of course, there were virtually no deployments during that year, so all of the unit moves appear as "move, not deploy," shown in the darkest segment of each bar. In the later years, the total number of interunit transfers is increasing (in both the M-2 and M-1 years relative to CY 2000), and the difference is due to the transfer of people from the source unit (which is heading toward deployment) into another unit with which they actually deploy—sometimes earlier (typically three to seven months) and sometimes later (15 to 20 months). In general, this paints a picture of increasing personnel turbulence, which is probably due in part to deliberate Army actions to cross-level individuals and in part to soldiers' decisions to move into other units with a later deployment date.

The case of the USAR truck companies is obviously an outlier in this picture, and it is instructive to examine the reasons why. For USAR truck units, interunit moves essentially doubled between CY 2000 and the M-2 and M-1 years, from 12 percent to 26 percent (M-2 year) and 23 percent (M-1 year). The excess moves in M-2 can be traced almost entirely to cross-leveling; of the 18 percent of unit membership that transferred to another deploying unit, fully 16 percentage points went to a unit with which those individuals deployed before their original unit. We interpret this as reflecting a crisis atmosphere in the USAR truck companies, in which some units that needed to deploy imminently were short of deployable soldiers. To meet the shortfall, the USAR transferred an appreciable number of soldiers out of units that

Figure 4.5
Interunit Moves, by Unit Type and Time Period

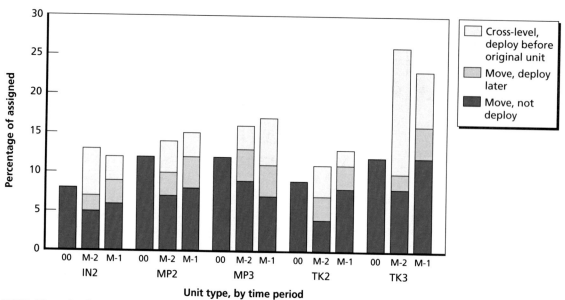

NOTE: 00 = calendar year 2000. M-2 = year from M – 24 months to M – 12 months. M-1 = year from M – 12 months to M-day.

were less than two years away from their own deployment into units that were preparing for a near-term deployment. Indeed, the extent of such scrambling can be seen in the fact that, even in units that were in the last year's run-up to mobilization (the lightest segment in the rightmost bar), 7 percent of the soldiers were transferred out to other units with which they deployed sooner.

Let us follow this story of the USAR trucks a little further. Figure 4.6 shows that they were unusual even in the base year, in that their personnel fill rates were lower than fill rates in other kinds of units. While the other four types of units enjoyed fill rates between 92 and 107 percent in CY 2000, the USAR truck units had a fill rate of only 82 percent. And later, as the demands for cross-leveling intensified when units were frequently called up, those fill rates dropped noticeably—down to 71 percent, on average, at M − 12 months.

Table 4.1 illustrates the challenge faced by the relatively sparsely filled USAR truck companies, compared with the more favorably situated ARNG infantry battalions. This table focuses entirely on cross-leveling and gains, ignoring other movements for the time being. At M − 24 months (24 months before mobilization), ARNG infantry battalions were filled to

Figure 4.6
Fill Rates, by Unit Type and Time Period

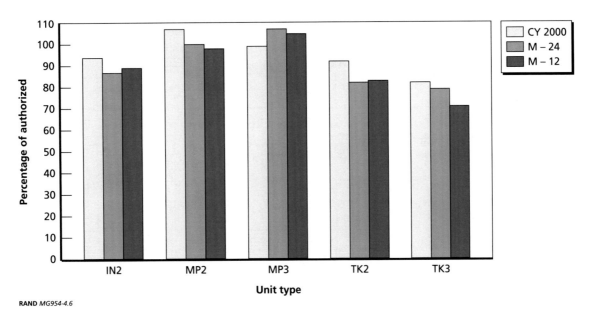

RAND *MG954-4.6*

Table 4.1
Fill Rates and Cross-Leveling Losses in Selected Unit Types

Item	Infantry Battalions (%)	USAR Truck Companies (%)
Fill at M − 24 months	87	79
Cross-leveling losses, M − 24 to M − 12	−8	−18
Fill remaining at M − 12	79	61
Gains, M − 24 to M − 12	10	10
Resulting fill, M − 12	89	71

87 percent of their authorized level. Not so for the USAR truck companies—they had a fill rate of only 79 percent. Then, over the next year, from M – 24 to M – 12, the infantry battalions lost soldiers amounting to 8 percent of their authorized strength as a result of cross-leveling actions. The USAR truck companies, by contrast, lost 18 percent because of cross-leveling during that same year. After those losses (ignoring other factors for the moment), the infantry battalions would stand at 79 percent of authorized, while the truck companies would stand at a mere 61 percent. Now in the same year, both types of units received gains of 10 percent of authorized strength. At the end of this process, at 12 months before mobilization, the infantry battalions would have 89 percent fill, while the truck companies would have only 71 percent.

This placed the truck companies in a strained posture, from which recovery would be quite difficult. How hard would it be to recover? Consider a hypothetical scenario: Suppose that the truck companies were extraordinarily successful in securing new people—say, through intensive recruiting of prior-service personnel combined with fast training of nonprior-service recruits—and suppose that those results doubled the gains, from 10 to 20 percent. Even so, their fill rate would still stand at only 81 percent.

Losses by Grade

Finally, let us consider the loss and move patterns for personnel of varying grades, as shown in Figure 4.7. This confirms the same pattern we saw in the overall stability statistics. Officer loss rates during the 12 months before mobilization were higher than those for junior enlisted personnel in all unit types, and notably higher than those for NCOs. The high loss rate for officers is a general pattern: Across the five unit types, officer loss rates ranged from 28 to 51 percent. Among NCOs, loss rates ranged from only 21 to 33 percent. What accounts for this difference?

The answer is provided in Figure 4.8, which breaks down losses into the categories that we examined earlier for the case of infantry battalions. Among junior enlisted personnel, the

Figure 4.7
Loss Rates for Officers, Noncommissioned Officers, and Junior Enlisted Personnel

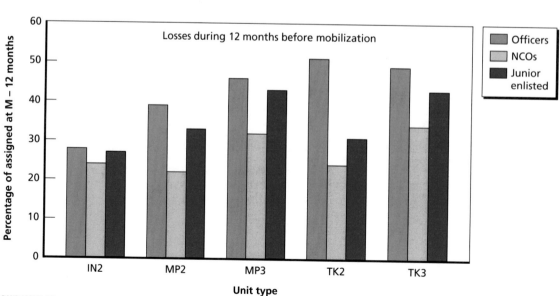

Figure 4.8
In Infantry Battalions, Most Officer Losses Come from Unit Moves; Junior Enlisted Losses Come from Leaving the Army

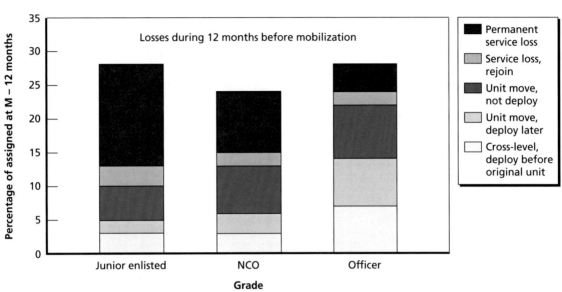

RAND *MG954-4.8*

predominant reason for loss was permanent departure from the Army. Among officers, in contrast, the predominant reason for loss was a unit move (22 percent of assigned), whereas service losses were relatively uncommon (6 percent of assigned). Compared with enlisted personnel, proportionately many more officers are cross-leveled into another unit that deploys earlier or into another unit with which they later deploy.

Figure 4.9 demonstrates that this pattern is not unique to the infantry battalions. In all five unit types, officer losses due to unit moves (the blue segments of the bars) far outweighed service losses (the red segments).

In fact, the dark blue segments—representing moves into a unit that did not deploy—account for the plurality of losses in all five unit types, markedly so in the MP and truck companies. Why are so many officers moving into nondeploying units? We do not have specific information on the reasons, but we can offer some possible explanations. First, recall that the rate of "move, not deploy" has been constant or decreasing over time (Figure 4.5)—unchanged even since 2000, when there were very few deployments of any kind. That suggests that many of these interunit moves are not induced by the prospect of upcoming deployment; instead, such moves are probably attributable to "normal" personnel movements. There can be many reasons for that kind of move. For example, a soldier may move to another unit for promotion (because the other unit has a vacancy at the next grade); to change specialties (for example, to move from infantry to another branch or vice versa); or to relocate to another community because of civilian employment opportunities or family reasons. The fact that the soldier's destination unit does not deploy could simply be the "luck of the draw"; that particular unit was not on a deployment schedule at the time. Alternatively, some of these moves could reflect an accommodation on the part of the Army, for an officer whose personal situation would create a hardship if deployed.

Thus, we see that a large aggregate loss rate breaks down into several different types of losses, each of which represents a different phenomenon. Each of the five outcomes in Figure 4.9

Figure 4.9
Most Officer Losses Reflect Interunit Moves

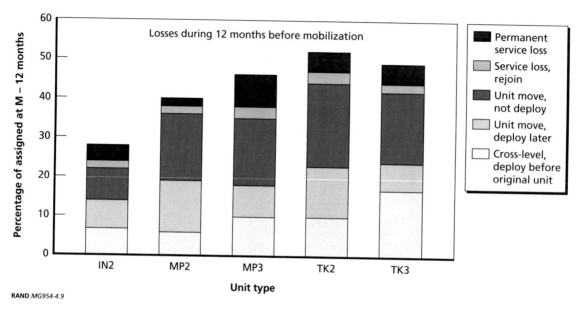

RAND *MG954-4.9*

is likely to be attributable to a different cause, and yet almost every one individually applies to only a small fraction of the unit's assigned personnel. To change loss rates, DoD would need one policy aimed at permanent losses, another at cross-leveling, another at unit moves without cross-leveling, and so forth. This suggests that there is no single "quick fix" to the loss problem.

CHAPTER FIVE

Nondeployers

Characteristics of Nondeployers

This chapter investigates the other major factor, beyond personnel losses, that leads to instability: soldiers who do not deploy even though they are assigned to the unit. Figure 5.1 displays the stability and deployment status of all unit members on D-day. Soldiers with 12 months or more in the unit represent a significant percentage of nondeployers—about half of them, as shown by the upper two segments of the bars in this figure. And nondeployers overall, regardless of tenure in the unit, account for about 30 percent of total unit strength on D-day.

Who are these nondeployers? Figure 5.2 shows nondeployment rates for officers, NCOs, and junior enlisted soldiers. In general, junior enlisted soldiers have the highest rates (about 30 to 50 percent of authorized).[1] However, many of the junior enlisted personnel are not legally deployable because they have not finished initial training (the light-green segments of the junior enlisted bars in Figure 5.2). When those "not qualified" personnel are removed, the

Figure 5.1
Deploying and Nondeploying Personnel, by Tenure in Unit

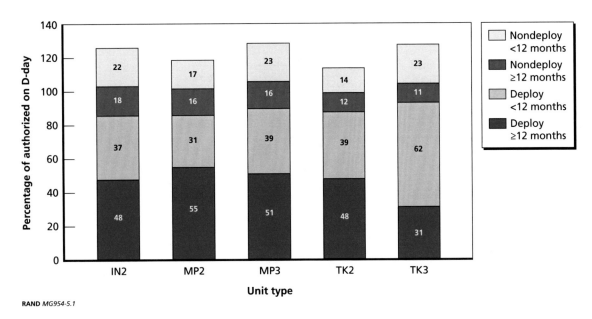

RAND *MG954-5.1*

---

[1] Note that these are percentages of *authorized positions*. Because units are normally overmanned at D-day, the nondeploying fraction of assigned personnel is lower. For example, the infantry units were manned at 124 percent of authorized, and 39 percent of authorized were nondeployers. Thus, about 31 percent of *assigned* personnel did not deploy.

Figure 5.2
Nondeployers, by Grade

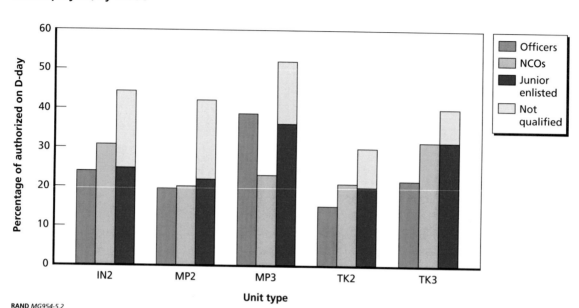

nondeployment rates for junior enlisted fall into the same general range as those for the NCOs and officers.[2]

Tracing Nondeployers After the Unit's Departure

What happened to soldiers who did not deploy? To answer that query, we subdivided the non-deployers into successively smaller groups as we had done in the analysis of losses. Figure 5.3 illustrates the results, again for infantry battalions. We begin at the left column, with all non-deployers represented as 100 percent. In the next column, that 100 percent of all nondeployers is broken into two primary groups: those who remained in the unit throughout our period of observation (66 percent) and those who left the unit (34 percent).

The third column, in the upper two boxes, further divides the stayers into those who deployed later (12 percent) and those who never deployed with their unit (54 percent).[3] In the lower boxes, those who left the unit are divided into soldiers who moved to another unit and those who left the service altogether.

Finally, the rightmost column breaks out several groups further. First, in the upper left is the distribution of the 54 percent who stayed in the unit but did not deploy during the period of observation. Among those, we find the following:

- Five percent were activated with the unit but did not deploy.

---

[2] A small number of officers have not completed initial education and training, but they account for only about 2 percent of nondeploying officers.

[3] Included in those who deployed later are some individuals who were initially unqualified but then completed initial military training and deployed with their original unit. They are counted within the upper "Deploy later" box (12 percent). In addition, some of the initially unqualified people moved to another unit and subsequently deployed (counted in the lower "Deploy later" box, marked 5 percent).

Figure 5.3
Army National Guard Infantry Battalions: What Happened to Soldiers Who Did Not Deploy?

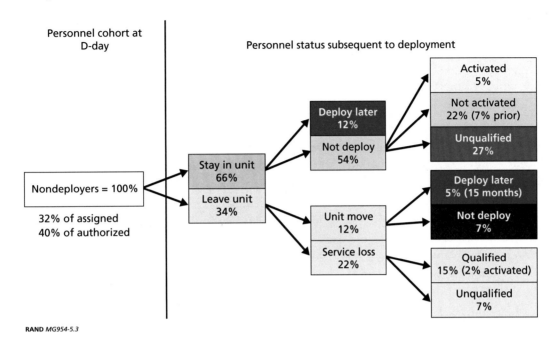

RAND *MG954-5.3*

- Twenty-two percent were not activated. But, among them, nearly one-third (7 percent) had a prior activation and therefore may not have been subject to redeployment at the time.
- Twenty-seven percent were not qualified (i.e., were untrained).

The second large group is made up of those who moved to another unit. Among those, we find the following:

- Five percent deployed later with another unit. On average, they deployed 15 months after their original unit deployed.[4]
- Seven percent did not deploy.

The third group includes those who left the service. Among them, we find the following:

- Fifteen percent were qualified for deployment. Among those, 2 percent had been activated by D-day but then left the service (on average, six months after the unit deployed). Some may have been found to be nondeployable after mobilization.
- Seven percent were not qualified.

---

[4] To determine this time lag, we tracked people beyond the one-year window after the source unit's deployment date. The fact of a move was determined by status at D + 12, but we looked further ahead to calculate the lag between D-day and the individual's deployment.

Loss and Move Rates for Nondeployers

The data in Figure 5.3 illustrate the picture only for infantry battalions. What does that picture look like for all unit types? It turned out that those patterns were replicated in all five unit types, in similar fashion, though not in exact proportions.

Nondeployers Who Left the Unit

Consider first Table 5.1, which represents soldiers who left the unit after it deployed. The first row includes personnel who left the service but had completed initial training and so were qualified to deploy.[5] The second row includes personnel who left the service but had not yet completed initial training when they left. Most likely, these are junior soldiers who dropped out of the unit before attending basic training or occupational skill training; our longitudinal data showed that approximately one-fourth of all new recruits drop out before completing initial training. On average, the people who became service losses left five to seven months after the unit deployed. We do not know their precise reasons for leaving, but, most likely, some were already approaching the expiration of their term of service and were not required to remain. Alternatively, some may have had medical or other conditions that made them non-deployable, but the system required time to process their discharge.

The total rate of service losses ranges around 21 percent of nondeployers. But recall that all nondeployers accounted for only a fraction of assigned personnel at the time the unit deployed (see Figure 5.1). The result is that service losses in this table represent only 5 to 7 percent of the unit's assigned personnel, not a major drain on the unit's strength.[6] And, of course, one should expect a certain amount of losses in any time period.

A somewhat more anomalous group appears in the third row of the table: those who moved to another unit but never deployed.[7] They represent from 7 to 22 percent of nondeploy-

Table 5.1
Post-Deployment Status of Soldiers Who Left the Unit After It Deployed

Status During Period After Deployment	Percentage of All Nondeployers				
	ARNG Infantry Battalions	ARNG MP Companies	USAR MP Companies	ARNG Truck Companies	USAR Truck Companies
Qualified service loss	15	13	18	18	15
Unqualified service loss	7	8	5	5	2
Unit move, nondeploy	7	7	15	8	22
Unit move, deploy	5	3	11	4	8

---

[5]   The entry in each row is a percentage of all nondeployers; the base includes persons represented in Tables 5.1 and 5.2.

[6]   For example, Table 5.1 shows that qualified and unqualified service losses in the infantry represent 22 percent of non-deployers. But nondeployers account for only 32 percent of assigned (Figure 5.1). So those service losses represent only about 7 percent of the unit's assigned personnel (0.32 × 0.22). The analogous calculations for other unit types produce rates between 5 and 7 percent.

[7]   We tracked those people through the end of our period of observation, which ended in 2008 and so covered a considerable period of time for most of these units.

ers, depending on the type of unit. On average, they moved to the new unit about five months after their original unit deployed.

In addition to those nondeploying movers, we also see, in the next row, another group of movers, those who went to another unit and deployed with it later during our period of observation. On average, those deployments occurred about 16 months after the original unit's deployment.

Together, the last two groups—interunit transfers—account for 10 to 12 percent of ARNG nondeployers and 26 to 30 percent of USAR nondeployers. As discussed in Chapter Four on personnel losses, we do not know the reasons for their moves. Some may have moved to another unit for promotion opportunity, to change specialty, or because of household moves. In those cases, the fact that the destination unit did not deploy may simply be fortuitous. In other cases, a move could represent the Army's accommodation to the personal circumstances of a unit member who preferred to deploy later and was permitted to move to another, later-deploying unit. In some cases, the soldier may have faced a severe hardship with deployment and the chain of command accepted a move to another nondeploying unit rather than lose the person entirely from the Army.

We interpret the higher rates of unit moves in the USAR to the generally turbulent atmosphere in the Army Reserve during this period. To enhance stability, the Army could consider instituting incentives or policies to keep people in units approaching deployment. We return to such policy-change scenarios in Chapter Seven.

Nondeployers Who Remained in the Unit

In each unit type, a notable segment of nondeployers remained in the unit after it left. Their behavior during the period after the unit's deployment is described in Table 5.2.

The first row includes soldiers who eventually deployed while assigned to their original unit, even though they had not deployed with the unit when the main body of troops departed. On average, they deployed about three to five months later than the unit. It seems likely that many of these soldiers had short-term constraints, such as a need to complete Army

Table 5.2
Post-Deployment Status of Soldiers Who Stayed in the Unit After It Deployed

Status	Percentage of All Nondeployers				
	ARNG Infantry Battalions	ARNG MP Companies	USAR MP Companies	ARNG Truck Companies	USAR Truck Companies
Deploy later with unit	13	7	8	12	6
Qualified, activated	5	7	6	8	8
Qualified, not activated	22	22	20	29	30
With prior deployment	7	5	6	8	17
With no prior deployment	15	17	14	21	13
Unqualified, remain in unit	27	33	17	17	7

schooling, temporary medical conditions, or family or employment situations that were later resolved, thus allowing them to join the unit in theater. They represent 6 to 13 percent of all nondeployers.

The second row includes soldiers who were activated with their unit but did not deploy, about 6 percent of all nondeployers. Most of them remained activated for about nine months. These could be part of a rear detachment, or some of them could have expected to deploy but were later found to have a condition that prevented it. They make up a small group, accounting for about 2 percent of unit strength.[8] It seems plausible that a group of that size could be performing coordination, liaison, and family support functions at the home station while the unit is overseas.

The third row is much larger—20 to 30 percent of all nondeployers—and seems anomalous at first inspection. They are soldiers who were not even activated, much less deployed, even though they had completed initial training and therefore were qualified for deployment. What could explain their failure to activate? One obvious explanation is the likelihood that the soldier had already been deployed, perhaps with another unit; under policies in effect during most of our observation period, soldiers with a prior recent activation were not required to activate and deploy again. As shown in the next row of the table, soldiers with a prior activation did account for a sizable subset of the nondeployers who were "qualified but not activated." On average, the prior activation had occurred 28 months before the unit's deployment—recently enough to suggest that redeploying the person could constitute a hardship. In the first four types of units, those with prior activations represented 25 to 35 percent of qualified nonactivated personnel. And, in the USAR truck companies, they represented more than half of the qualified nonactivated.

The problem of prior deployments points to a complication that can affect all units, even those that have not recently deployed. As soldiers move through the system, they bring their personal deployment history with them. Because DoD guidelines govern deployment of individuals and not just units, some people who have moved into the unit may not be available for deployment because they have had an earlier deployed tour. This type of turbulence carries implications for assessing personnel availability within the unit readiness reporting system.

Other possible explanations lie in additional criteria that make a person "not available for deployment," as defined by Army readiness reporting procedures (see U.S. Department of the Army, 2006). Such criteria include medical conditions and legal and administrative reasons that preclude a soldier's deployment even though he or she has completed all necessary individual training and qualification processes.[9] The sum of such groups often reaches 5 percent or more of a unit's strength, according to aggregate readiness summaries. That is consistent with the observed number of the remaining nondeployers shown here. For example, for infantry

---

[8]   Recall that nondeployers represent only about 30 percent of unit strength at the time the unit deploys. Thus, the fraction of all unit members is 0.06×0.30, or about 2 percent.

[9]   For example, some soldiers may be found to have a chronic medical condition or a permanent or temporary profile that precludes deployment. In addition, some soldiers may be not available for legal or administrative reasons: because of pending administrative or disciplinary action, investigation, unsatisfactory participation, or "simultaneous membership" in another program, such as Reserve Officer Training Corps (ROTC), from which a cadet will not be withdrawn. The occurrence rates of these conditions in readiness reports provide a baseline for comparisons, even though personnel deployment decisions in an actual operation may be governed by more specific Army policies or command guidance relevant to the particular theater or contingency.

battalions, the qualified nonactivated with no prior deployments represent about 5 percent of the unit.[10]

The fourth and final group is composed of soldiers who were unqualified (i.e., had not yet completed initial training) but remained in the unit. The presence of such a group is not surprising. All RC units contain new nonprior-service recruits who are awaiting basic training or skill training. Since the Army does not generally provide a separate account to hold these trainees, they are charged against the unit's strength. They often account for 6 to 10 percent of overall unit strength, which is in the range observed here. Among these untrained personnel who stayed in the unit, nearly 60 percent in the ARNG and 80 percent in the USAR did complete their initial training within one year.

Stepping back from this complex picture, we make one important observation: There are many distinct causes of nondeployment, and each of them reflects only a modest fraction of the total unit membership. A soldier can be on his or her way out of the service (permanent loss), move to another unit, deploy later with his or her unit, be activated but kept behind at home station, be nondeployable for various reasons prescribed in regulations, or be waiting for initial entry training. All of these conditions, when summed together, make up a sizable group, but, individually, each is small. In Chapter Seven, we return to that point as we examine the potential for policy changes that might help reduce the prevalence of nondeployers in RC units.

---

[10] An approximate calculation is (0.15 with no prior deployments) × 0.32 = 0.048.

CHAPTER SIX

Effects of Instability on Training

The preceding analysis establishes that RC units experience considerable personnel instability, even during the run-up to deployment. The instability is present across many different types of units and senior as well as junior personnel, and it arises from numerous separate causes. Now we examine the potential effects of that instability on training, as the unit prepares for mobilization and deployment.

RC units have always faced challenges in training before mobilization, for a variety of reasons. Many units begin the process undermanned; some of the personnel who are present have not completed initial entry training; and, during the normal course of a year, RC units have limited time to train together (normally, 39 days per year, including 12 weekends a month and a two-week AT period). In addition, on average, only about 60 to 70 percent of the unit's members are able to attend AT.[1]

Despite these limitations, the run-up to deployment must include much training for individuals, including practice on basic warrior skills and theater-specific training prescribed by the combatant command. The unit must also conduct collective training for crews, platoons, and companies (and even more collective events if the unit contains higher-echelon formations). Yet, at the same time, everyone wants to keep the post-mobilization period as short and efficient as possible, to maximize BOG time for the unit in theater.[2] The DoD policy limiting the mobilization period to 12 months further intensified the pressure to get everything done before mobilization.

To respond, Army RC units have recently been planning intensive AT and IDT training over an entire year before mobilization. For example, some units have planned and executed multiple AT periods distributed across the entire pre-mobilization year. However, as we have just seen, unit personnel are not stable during the period before mobilization. In this chapter, we show how this instability unfolds as many new arrivals join the unit, spread over many months before mobilization. This instability potentially undercuts the effectiveness of extended pre-mobilization training, because new arrivals miss training events that have occurred before they join. As a result, units must repeat some training either before or after mobilization, slowing preparation and potentially requiring a longer post-mobilization training period. First, we

---

[1] See, for example, Sortor et al. (1994) for the results of Army attempts to enhance training of high-priority units in the aftermath of the first Persian Gulf War.

[2] In fact, post-mobilization periods have shortened over time since the first deployments in 2003. For example, since the advent of the operational reserve policy, the post-mobilization training time for brigades has been shortened, from four months or more to three months or less.

review the data to describe the buildup of personnel in a deploying unit, and then we draw some inferences about the effects on pre-mobilization training schedules.

When Do New Deploying Members Join the Unit?

Figure 6.1 illustrates the buildup of unit personnel for ARNG infantry battalions that deployed between 2003 and 2008. It portrays the growth of personnel in the unit inventory for two types of personnel: soldiers who were assigned to the unit on D-day (the upper, solid line) and soldiers who eventually deployed with the unit on D-day (the lower, dashed line).

This figure presents a retrospective picture—looking backward from D-day to when each soldier arrived in the unit. The points on the lines show the percentages of authorized personnel among those who were in the unit on D-day (the y-axis), according to the length of time they had been in the unit before D-day (the x-axis). For example, consider the upper solid line. It shows the buildup trend for all personnel who were assigned to the unit on D-day. At the month when the unit deployed, the number of personnel assigned represented 124 percent of the unit's authorized strength. Accordingly, the solid line intercepts the "0 month" (right margin) at 124 percent. In contrast, at the point 12 months before deployment (left margin), the number that was assigned at $D - 12$ and still assigned to the unit on D-day represented only 68 percent of authorized strength.

The lower dashed line shows a comparable buildup pattern for personnel who eventually deployed with the unit. At the month when the unit deployed, its deploying soldiers represented 85 percent of the unit's authorized strength. Thus, the dashed line intercepts the

Figure 6.1
Army National Guard Infantry Battalions: When New Unit Arrivals and Deployers Joined the Unit

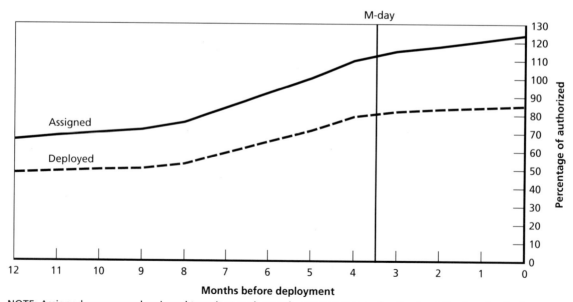

NOTE: Assigned = personnel assigned to unit at each month, as percentage of authorized. Deployed = deployers assigned to unit at each month, as percentage of authorized.
RAND *MG954-6.1*

"0 month" (right margin) at 85 percent.[3] In contrast, at the point 12 months before deployment (left margin), soldiers who were present in the unit and who eventually deployed with the unit represented only 49 percent of authorized strength. Intermediate points can be read in the same way; for example, at 6 months before deployment, the unit contained eventual deployers who represented 67 percent of authorized.

Inspecting this picture reveals some important facts about the speed of the personnel buildup. First, new members start to arrive in quantity about eight months before D-day. That is the point at which both lines begin to slope upward at a more rapid pace. Second, the unit rapidly builds up personnel until the mobilization point—here, depicted as about 3.5 months before deployment. After that, the pace of new arrivals slackens, particularly among eventual deployers.

As a result, about 95 percent of the deployers were in place by the mobilization point (0.81/0.85). There was some ongoing instability because some new people were still arriving, even after mobilization. However, those new arrivals were small numbers relative to the group that eventually deployed, and so they probably had little effect on the complexity or timing of post-mobilization training.

Finally, notice that many of those who eventually deployed were in fact "new arrivals" in the unit. Out of the group that deployed, nearly one-fourth had arrived since D − 6 months, and nearly half had arrived since D − 12 months. The continuing arrival of new people, many of whom will eventually deploy with the unit, spells instability within the unit and limits the amount of training that can be done far in advance of deployment.

Training Schedules

To see concretely how this instability affects the scheduling and feasibility of training, we examined training programs for various types of units, including the infantry, MP, and truck units that were the focus of this study. We attended several pre-mobilization planning conferences arranged by First Army, in which soon-to-mobilize units presented and discussed their training plans and milestones in preparation for their upcoming deployments. Here, we display samples of those training programs and compare them with the empirically observed buildup curves for the corresponding unit type.

Infantry Training

Figure 6.2 displays the average infantry battalion buildup curve for deployers (the solid line) together with the training plan for a particular ARNG infantry brigade. The brigade's plan included several key training events, as shown by the vertical bars spaced over the 12-month period before deployment. For example, the brigade conducted a combat training center (CTC)–like event over a two-week period about 11 months before D-day. Later, over a period of successive months, it conducted training on improvised explosive devices (IEDs), a brigade

Figure 6.2
Sample 2008 Army National Guard Brigade Combat Team Training Plan Compared with Typical Buildup of Deploying Personnel

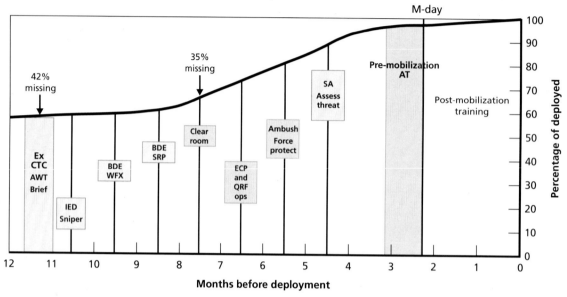

NOTE: Ex CTC = externally supported combat training center event. AWT = Army Warrior Training (individual skills required of all soldiers). Brief = mandatory briefings (e.g., theater orientation, health, harassment). IED = improvised explosive device training. BDE = brigade. WFX = warfighter exercise. SRP = soldier readiness program (e.g., individual preparation, wills, family support plan, medical screening). ECP = entry control-point operations. QRF = quick-reaction force. SA = situational awareness. Ops = operations.
RAND *MG954-6.2*

warfighter exercise, training on clearing rooms and protecting against ambush, and so forth, culminating in an AT period just before mobilization.

But notice how the buildup curve of eventual deployers compares with those training events. At month D – 11, when the unit was undergoing its CTC event, only about 58 percent of the eventual deployers were in the unit. Therefore, that event was missed by the other 42 percent of deployers who arrived later.

Similarly, the training on room clearance, occurring about month D – 7, came at a time when only 65 percent of deployers had joined the unit. The remaining 35 percent who later joined the unit would have missed that event.[4] In general, it is clear that, whenever training events are stretched out over a period of 12 months or more before mobilization, those training events will not affect a large proportion of the soldiers who go to war with the unit.

Military Police Company Training

As shown in Figure 6.3, MP companies present a similar problem. This figure compares the average personnel buildup curve for MP companies with the timing of key training events for a sample ARNG MP company in 2008.

---

[4] We recognize that some incoming soldiers may have experienced some of the same training, particularly individual training, in the source unit from which they were transferred. But Army policies often impose a time limit specifying recency of the training. In addition, because threats and conditions in theater are continually evolving, any training that the soldier had received many months earlier might not be complete or up to date. And, when the unit conducts collective training, commanders prefer to have all soldiers present.

Figure 6.3
Sample 2008 Army National Guard Military Police Company Training Plan Compared with Typical Buildup of Deploying Personnel

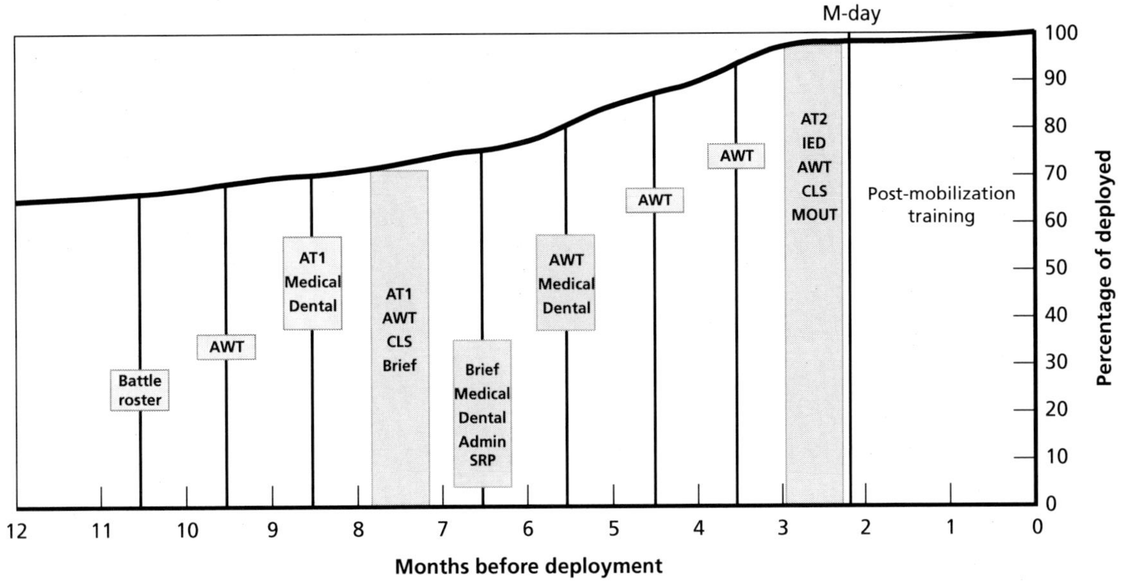

NOTE: CLS = combat lifesaver training. MOUT = military operations in urban terrain.
RAND MG954-6.3

Once again, it can be seen that the early part of the buildup period included several important training events—such as individual Army Warrior Training (common battlefield tasks), a two-week AT that included combat lifesaver training, and medical and dental examinations and procedures. The timing of those events meant that 20 to 30 percent of the company's eventual deployers would miss them, because that percentage joined the unit after the event. In this case, the MP company scheduled its major collective training assembly just before mobilization: the event marked "AT2," which included training on IEDs, combat lifesaver training, and military operations in urban terrain. Since the inflow of deployers was nearly complete by that AT2 event (month D − 3), those important collective training tasks would have been experienced by almost all of the people who deployed with the unit.

Truck Companies

Figure 6.4 presents the analogous picture for USAR truck companies. Notice that the truck units have a steep buildup curve. At D − 8 months, only 40 percent of the eventual deployers were in the unit; thereafter, the personnel inflow proceeded quickly, so that the unit was nearly filled with deployers by D − 3 months. To cope with that, this truck company squeezed most of its training events into the short period just before mobilization. Nonetheless, given this plan, the IED training (at D − 6 months) would have been missed by 40 percent of the eventual deployers, and even AT2 would have been missed by about 14 percent of them. Moreover, that 14 percent is probably an understatement; we know that AT attendance rates often run in the range of 60 to 70 percent, so many of the soldiers who were assigned to the unit may have missed the AT event anyway.

Figure 6.4
Sample 2008 U.S. Army Reserve Truck Company Training Plan Compared with Typical Buildup of Deploying Personnel

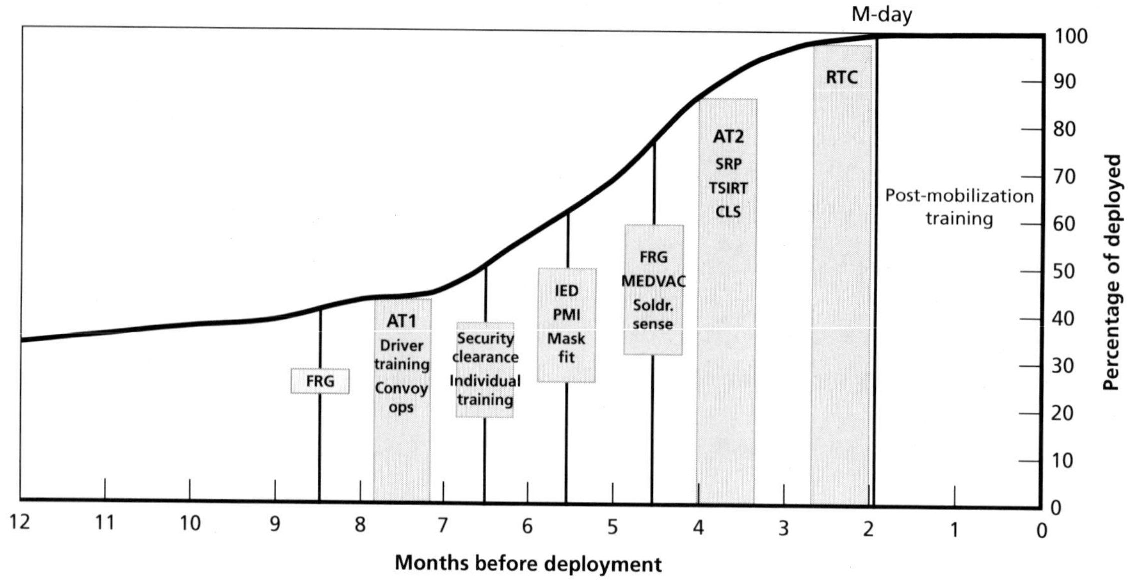

NOTE: FRG = family readiness group. PMI = preventive maintenance and inspections. MEDVAC = medical evacuation. Soldr. sense = soldier-as-sensor training (e.g., detecting threats). TSIRT = theater-specific individual readiness training. RTC = Reserve Training Center.

RAND MG954-6.4

Recent Changes in Buildup Curves

Another possible trend bears mentioning: It appears that personnel buildup curves have become steeper in recent years, although the evidence so far is not conclusive.

Figure 6.5 shows the buildup curve for deployers in ARNG infantry battalions, divided into two time periods: (1) units that deployed in 2003 through 2005 (the dashed line) and (2) units that deployed in 2006 through 2008 (the solid line). Notice that, in the earlier period, about 60 percent of eventual deployers were in the unit at D − 12 months. However, the later units had less than 50 percent in the unit at that point. Both eventually converge later, but the more–recently deploying units have a steeper curve. That means that, for the first half of the pre-mobilization year, the percentage of deployers who are present in the unit is even lower in recent years than it was during the earlier years.

As of this writing, we have only about ten deploying infantry battalions in the database for the period 2006–2008. However, they include a large enough number of individuals to give these statistics fairly good precision (there are 670 to 700 authorized positions in each battalion).

The data for MP and truck companies show a similar pattern: increasingly steep curves in the recent past. Therefore, we suspect that the trend is robust. However, the number of deploying units in recent years is sufficiently small that they might have some unique characteristics or be unrepresentative. Therefore, only with the passage of time and more deployments can it be determined whether the steeper curve is a stable phenomenon.

Figure 6.5
Personnel Buildup Curves for Two Time Periods: 2003–2005 and 2006–2008, Army National Guard Infantry Battalions

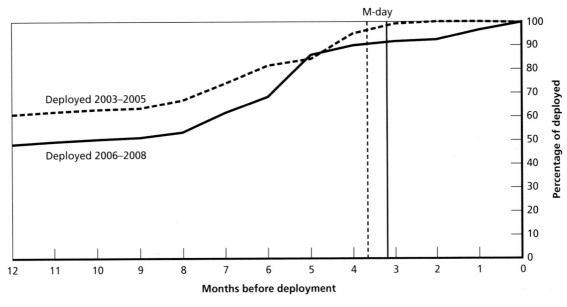

RAND *MG954-6.5*

What Instability Means for Training

These findings have some important overall implications for training RC units. First, all types of units show steep buildup curves during the last six to eight months before mobilization. That means that many soldiers—up to half of all deployers, those who enter during the last few months—will miss certain pre-mobilization training events.

That fact has cascading effects on subsequent training. For those soldiers who were not present in the unit when the previous training occurred, the training will have to be repeated, either before or after mobilization. If it occurs after mobilization—when virtually all of the deployers will be present—the unit faces a risk of lengthening the post-mobilization training period and eating into BOG time. If it occurs before mobilization, the unit will be scrambling to repeat several classes and training exercises as new arrivals flow in, and it will need the attendant resources to repeat that training. Many units, in fact, schedule makeup training later in the pre-mobilization period.

As it is, pre-mobilization training frequently requires substantial resources that are external to the unit. For example, the National Guard has Provisional Training Assistance Elements (PTAEs) that are controlled by the state headquarters and that provide help to the deploying unit. Those elements are sized at one PTAE member for every 60 soldiers being mobilized, so they represent an appreciable investment of resources. Similarly, the Army Reserve operates three RTCs that are semipermanent entities containing about 100 people who support training for deploying units. Both of these kinds of training support—along with First Army and its subordinate elements—are needed to accomplish theater-specific instruction, pre-deployment administration, medical and dental procedures, certification, and other tasks in preparation for the unit's deployment. To the extent that training events must be repeated, the Army must plan to invest more in these external training support activities.

The attendance rate at AT also affects the training process. Many units have reacted to the accelerated schedules by instituting extended or multiple AT periods (e.g., ATs that are 21 days rather than 15 days long, or ATs repeated two or three times within the last year before mobilization). However, attendance rates at AT have historically ranged around 60 to 70 percent, and, the more time they take, the greater the risk that some soldiers will not attend. Therefore, increasing the length or number of ATs probably has limits, complicated by the rapid inflow of new personnel.[5]

Finally, there are limitations on units' ability to work around instability by scheduling major training events just before mobilization. Frequently, units have left just one or two weeks separating the final training events and mobilization, and, by doing so, they ensured that most deploying soldiers participated. However, that cannot always be done because of constraints on training areas and resources (such as RTCs), which have a fixed capacity and may not be able to handle several units at once.

Despite these caveats, recent history records two important points on the positive side. First, 95 percent of deployers are in place by the mobilization point. Therefore, however complex or chaotic pre-mobilization training may be, post-mobilization training can be done fairly efficiently. Second, during the entire period of deployments since 2003, no units have missed or significantly slipped their planned arrival date in theater.[6] That experience demonstrates that units were able to complete training that was deemed essential by the command structure—but at the cost of some scrambling.

---

[5] Before embarking on an attempt to improve AT attendance, DoD should assess recent and current attendance rates to see whether they are markedly different from historical rates (such as those reported in Sortor et al., 1994). Attendance could be more problematic now, if intensified demands for pre-mobilization training have resulted in longer AT or IDT periods. If attendance does prove to be a problem, then DoD could consider instituting an incentive program to increase attendance rates and testing its effectiveness.

[6] The unit's ability to meet its planned arrival date indicates that it was deemed to be trained to standard, within the planned time frame, before deployment. It refers primarily to completion of pre-deployment training: For example, soldiers were trained to standard on those skills required by the theater commander and were available to the theater on the required date. However, it does not say anything about their in-theater performance. There is no systematic assessment mechanism for actual mission performance, and, in fact, the mission requirements vary widely; those two facts make it difficult to say much about actual combat performance.

CHAPTER SEVEN

Policy Directions and Options

In spite of the record of unit success in training and deploying on time, many military experts are troubled by the continuing amount of personnel instability in units—and particularly in units that are about to go to war. Numerous observers have related examples of the challenges, inefficiencies, and extra effort required to cope with instability in a time-stressed training environment. Therefore, we wanted to examine the prospects for potential policy changes that might improve the level of personnel stability in deploying units.

Gauging Effects of Potential Policy Changes to Reduce Instability

The first thing to note is that many different sources contributed to instability in deploying units. Here, we recapitulate some key facts adduced in previous sections and use them to structure an analysis of the possible payoffs from constraining various sources of personnel turbulence.

The primary drivers of instability fall into two categories. One category is personnel losses, which arise from three major factors:

- permanent losses (departure from service)
- unit moves
- cross-leveling into other deploying units.

Nondeploying personnel constitute the other major source. We identified four major classes of personnel who do not deploy:

- unqualified (soldiers lacking initial training, who cannot be deployed)
- activated, but not deployed
- not activated, with a prior activation
- not activated, with no prior activation.

In this chapter, we address the question for each of these sources of instability: How much might policy changes reduce instability? The logic will proceed as follows:

- First, we consider which sources of instability could feasibly be constrained.
- Then, we posit certain levels of improvement in the various sources (e.g., reducing losses from the service, cutting the number of unqualified soldiers).

- Using reasonable assumptions about the magnitude of those improvements, we then calculate the fraction of the unit's deployers who would be "stable" soldiers (those who have been in the unit for one year or more).

Infantry Units: An Example

Let us begin with the example of infantry battalions. As we have seen, infantry units face a large gap between the number of stable soldiers and the number needed to deploy. Figure 7.1 displays the typical situation for infantry (averaged across all the battalions in our sample). At the bottom of the figure is the "stable" group, shown in orange. They are the soldiers who deployed with the unit on its D-day and had more than one year's tenure in the unit at that time. Under current circumstances, this group constitutes only 47 percent of authorized. Yet, the unit deployed with 85 percent of authorized. The Army presumably would like that entire 85 percent to be soldiers who were stable in the unit. The current situation therefore leaves a "gap"—shown by the vertical arrow at the right—of 38 percent: 85 percent who must deploy minus the 47 percent who are stable.

How could the Army increase the stable group? In our data for infantry battalions, we identified two unstable groups whose numbers conceivably might be reduced:

- *stable nondeployers:* soldiers who did not deploy but had at least one year tenure in the unit (the middle, yellow segment of the bar)
- *losses:* soldiers who had been in the unit at D − 12 months but who left the unit during the ensuing year (the upper, blue segment).

The objective of policy change, therefore, would be to reduce the size of the yellow and blue groups by converting them into stable deployers. That is, policy would aim to reduce losses

Figure 7.1
Gap Between Number of Stable Soldiers and Number Needed to Deploy (Army National Guard Infantry Battalions)

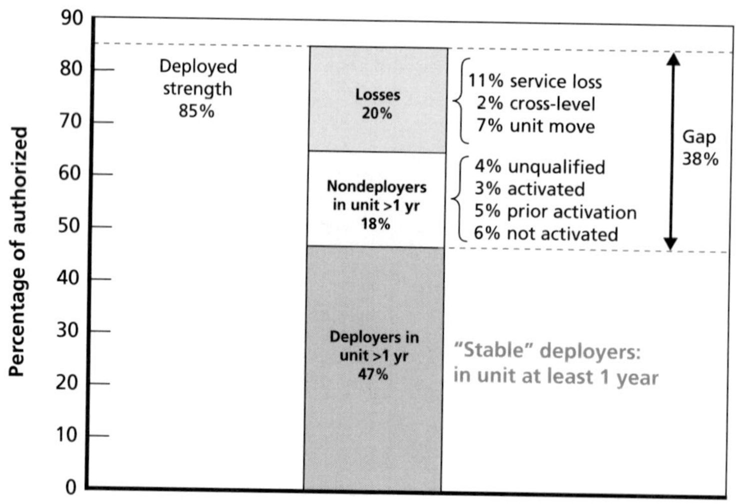

among those who were present at D − 12 and to convert the long-tenure nondeployers into deployers.

Detailed reasons for instability are shown in black at the right, next to the two braces. Each reason represents a specific number of people who were affected by it. For example, within the loss group, 11 percent of authorized were service losses; 2 percent left the unit by cross-leveling into another unit that deployed earlier; and 7 percent moved to another unit but did not deploy. The issue is this: How much would the figure of 47 percent stable rise if the Army were able to reduce some of these causes? To address that issue, we ask this question: Which reasons might plausibly be changed by policy, and what level of effect might we expect?

Figure 7.2 shows the answers that we derived. The left-hand bar is the same base case as before, labeled "Recent experience." The right-hand bar ("With policy changes") represents our calculation of the outcomes if various causes of instability were addressed by policy initiatives. The overall answer is that policy changes might reduce the gap somewhat but not eliminate it. Under our assumptions, at best, the percentage of the unit that was stable unit members and deployers would rise by 14 percentage points, leaving a gap of 24 percent. Here are the assumptions about possible policies and their effects that underlie that calculation:

- Reduce service losses by one-fourth, which would mean a sizable increase in retention. The 11-percent service losses would be cut by 3 percentage points.
- Maintain cross-leveling at 2 percent, because this level was based on deliberate Army decisions giving priority to other units.
- Control unit moves, reducing them by about half. That would reduce the 7-percent unit-move rate by 4 percentage points.
- Accelerate initial entry training for all unqualified soldiers, saving 4 percentage points that would otherwise have been nondeployers.
- Take no action on the 3 percent who were activated but not deployed, and continue to excuse from deployment those soldiers with recent activations.

Figure 7.2
Effects of Possible Policy Changes: Army National Guard Infantry Battalions

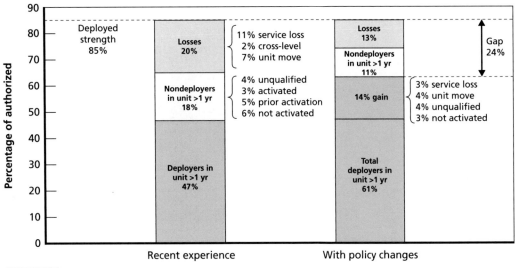

- Reduce the number of soldiers not activated by half, cutting that group by 3 percentage points.

As shown in the orange portion of the right-hand bar, those policy effects would convert a total of 14 percent (of authorized) from losses or nondeployers into stable deployers. Adding those 14 percent to the stable group would increase the total group of stable deployers to 61 percent of authorized. But even so, that would leave a gap of 24 percent between the stable group and the 85 percent who must deploy—a gap that would have to be filled by new arrivals.

Truck Companies: A Comparison Example

Now let us again contrast the USAR truck companies against the ARNG infantry battalions. Recall that the USAR truck companies had experienced a particularly high rate of cross-leveling losses to other units in year M-2. As illustrated in the left portion of Figure 7.3, cross-leveling losses in those companies were far greater than in any other unit type. As a result, at the end of year M-2, the USAR truck companies had a fill rate well below the other unit types, as shown in the right portion of the figure. Therefore, when the time came to deploy, the USAR truck companies had many more vacancies to fill in order to reach their target deployment level.

The situation of the USAR truck companies at D-day is displayed in Figure 7.4. Those companies deployed with less than one-third stable members: the 29 percent depicted in the orange segment at the bottom of the bar. What caused the deployment of so many people in the "unstable" category? There were three reasons: vacancies (the gray segment), losses (the blue segment), and nondeployers who had been in the unit more than one year (the yellow segment). Again, the figure shows, on the right next to the braces, the detailed categories of conditions that caused these results.

Figure 7.3
Low Fill Rates in U.S. Army Reserve Truck Companies

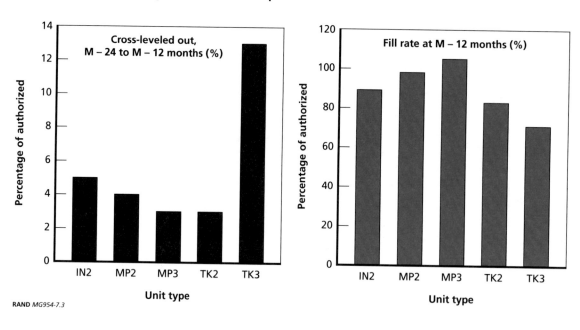

Figure 7.4
U.S. Army Reserve Truck Companies: Fewer Than One-Third
Stable Members Deployed

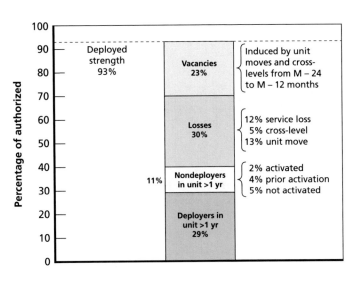

RAND *MG954-7.4*

The principal difference between this picture and its analogue for infantry battalions lies in the relatively low fill rates in USAR truck units, influenced by previous cross-leveling. Because those units had proportionately fewer soldiers, the three groups at the lower portion of the chart were also smaller. The stable deployers amounted to only 29 percent of authorized; stable nondeployers amounted to 11 percent; and losses among personnel who had been in the unit 12 months before deployment amounted to 30 percent. (Of course, there were other personnel in the unit, and many of them deployed, but they had not been in the unit at D – 12 and therefore would not be stable even if they deployed.)

The challenge of this situation can be appreciated by comparing the percentage of stable deployers (29 percent) with the actual fill rate of the unit when it deployed (93 percent, which we take to be the target level). Thus, there was a 64-percent gap between the percentage of authorized personnel who are deploying troops and the percentage who are stable deployers.

Indeed, even if the yellow and blue groups could be eliminated, the unit would still lack some stable deployers. Adding the yellow and blue groups, assuming that all of them could be retained and turned into deployers, would create a stable cohort that made up only 70 percent of authorized. Yet, the unit actually deployed at 93 percent of authorized. Therefore, vacancies accounted for at least a 23-percentage-point difference between the upper bound of achievable stable personnel and the target fill rate at deployment: 93 percent versus 70 percent.

So how much might that gap be closed if the Army instituted aggressive policies to create a more stable force? Figure 7.5 exhibits the potential result under our assumptions. Once again, we assume that the Army might reduce losses by one-fourth, unit moves by more than half, and those not activated by one half. After those improvements, total losses would shrink by 11 percentage points and stable nondeployers by 2 percentage points.

Those results would increase the percentage of stable deployers from 29 to 42 percent. Recall, though, that the unit actually deployed at 93-percent strength. The difference would have to be made up by new arrivals, meaning a gap of 51 percentage points between the goal (a fully stable deploying unit) and what could reasonably be expected. Therefore, in the case of

Figure 7.5
U.S. Army Reserve Truck Companies: Feasible Policy Changes Still Leave a Large Gap

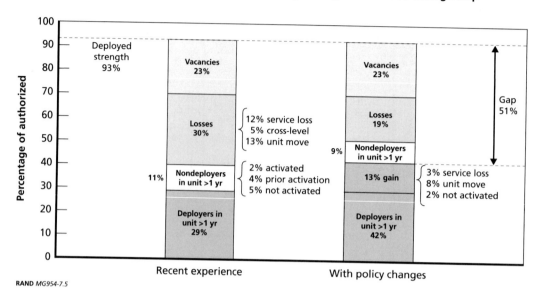

RAND *MG954-7.5*

USAR truck companies even more so than the case of infantry battalions, the deploying units would experience considerable personnel instability.

Once again, we see that a large aggregate loss rate breaks down into several different subgroups, each of which represents a different phenomenon. Therefore, DoD would need different policies to affect each one of them. Moreover, in both of the examples just discussed, only small numbers attach to each subgroup that shifted from losses or nondeployers into stable deployers. For example, cutting service losses yielded a change of only 3 percent of the unit's authorizations. Even reducing unit moves yielded only 8 percent. These percentages are small compared with the size of the gap the unit originally faced. It seems unlikely that all of the necessary policies would be adopted and that each would be successful at the levels we assumed, so the results we depicted in Figures 7.2 and 7.5 really represent an optimistic "best case." Because of those considerations, we conclude that there is no single "quick fix" to the instability problem, and, in fact, it is likely to persist as it has in the past.

Adapting to Continuing Instability: Policy Options

These analyses suggest that even determined Army interventions are not likely to sharply reduce instability in RC units. Even with multiple policy interventions, a large gap will remain between the number of stable soldiers and a unit's targeted deploying strength. Therefore, most units will need a large influx of new arrivals to reach desired strength at the time of deployment, and pre-deployment training will have to adapt to continuing instability.

Given that instability, what options may be considered to manage training and balance the Army's diverse goals? We suggest four alternatives.

Continue Current Policy, Which Is to Stretch Training over Many Months
The Army could continue to stretch out training events over a considerable period before mobilization. Recent training plans typically schedule many events over a 12-month period,

including intensive training activities, such as extended or multiple AT assemblies. In addition, according to some plans we have seen, further training events may be scheduled over the entire preceding year—that is, the period of stepped-up training would cover two years before the unit's anticipated deployment. To reduce personnel turbulence and unit losses during such a long period, the Army might increase retention bonuses or attempt to place controls on personnel movements (such as moves to another unit). However, we would not anticipate appreciable improvements in loss rates. Unit-loss rates of 20 to 30 percent per year have held up over several decades. As we have seen, most of these movements are not permanent departures from the Army. Actually, the rate of service losses seems rather low (averaging 12 percent per year). Most of the losses from a given unit arise from soldier transfers to other units.

Moreover, further attempts to control interunit transfers might backfire. RC soldiers can always discontinue participation. Confronted with a requirement to remain in the unit, some soldiers would probably leave the Army altogether. In this situation, the Army may simply need to accept existing rates of instability, the necessity for repeated training of new arrivals, and attendant risks to deployment timelines. If those burdens appear too great, the Army might consider incentives or other measures to minimize losses. If so, it would be wise to conduct preliminary small-scale experiments to test the value of those measures, such as larger retention bonuses aimed at keeping people in the service and in the unit.

Cluster Training Just Before Mobilization

A second option, favored by some units whose training plans we have reviewed, would be to cluster most training events in the last few months before mobilization. Such a program would take advantage of the fact that units have received 75 to 80 percent of their deployers by about D − 5 months. Intensive training could be concentrated during those last few months just before mobilization and a brief post-mobilization training period before the unit deploys. If necessary, incentives could be offered to ensure that those soldiers remain in the unit over the desired time period.

However, the clustered training plan also entails greater burdens on the soldier, family, and employer during the immediate pre-mobilization period. In some cases, units have scheduled their final AT just before mobilization, with a gap of only a few days to a few weeks. To some, this looks very much like an extended mobilization period, which was what the new DoD policy was intended to avoid. If this option were to be considered for widespread adoption, it would be wise to ascertain the true attitudes of soldiers, families, and employers about the relative burdens they perceive in this type of program compared with the others. And again, if DoD wants to get conclusive data on the behavioral reactions of soldiers (e.g., retention or transfer into other units), it could mount an experiment in selected units and compare the results with those in a matched set of units that do not participate.

Increase the Duration of Mobilization

A more direct way of compressing training into the last stages before deployment would be to defer some training until mobilization and increase the length of the mobilization period. This is in fact what was done during the period before 2007, when soldiers were mobilized for more than 12 months to accommodate extended pre-deployment training. Even today, something similar happens with some units. Suppose that the unit does intense training during the last month before mobilization (say, in a rotation to an RTC or an extended AT), and, thereafter, its post-mobilization training requires one month. That pattern conforms to some recent training plans for support units. Under current policy limiting mobilization to 12 months, that leaves 11 months BOG time (discounting time for travel to and from theater and for transfer of control among units). If the mobilization period were lengthened to 13 months, the post-mobilization period could cover the unit's entire two-month period of intensive training (the previous one month at the RTC/AT and the previous one-month post-mobilization training). BOG time would remain constant at 11 months.

Such a program has both pros and cons. On the plus side, it guarantees that the unit's members are all together for key training events, and it avoids possible skill decay and forgetting newly acquired knowledge. It also provides full benefits and continuity status for pay and allowances for the unit's soldiers during their final months of intensive training. On the other hand, such a practice would require relaxation of the constraints in recently declared DoD policy, which limits mobilization to 12 months. And, since it would officially mobilize RC soldiers for longer periods, it would probably be contentious and impose both budget and political costs upon DoD and the services.

Reduce Boots-on-the-Ground Time

A fourth option would be to push the most-intensive training into the post-mobilization period, as in option 3, but keep the length of mobilization constant at 12 months. That alternative has the same training advantages as option 3 but avoids disadvantages of lengthening mobilization. However, it obviously would reduce BOG time. For example, in the case of a support unit, if post-mobilization training took two months instead of one month as in the previous example, BOG time would drop from 11 to ten months. For combat brigades, a similar plan would probably reduce BOG time to approximately eight months. It would also lead to a slightly faster "spin rate" in theater, since each unit would stay for a shorter length of time. On the other hand, Marine Corps units have long employed a rotation period of only seven months (Garamone, 2009), so there is some precedent, and that system seems to have worked well enough to be maintained over a long period of time.

We cannot recommend one of these options in preference to another, other than to outline the pros and cons as we have done in this section. Each has significant advantages and disadvantages that need to be weighed by policymakers. If these or other alternatives are to be considered and analyzed in the future, we would suggest three key criteria to be taken into account:

- stability of trainees during key training periods
- amount of retraining required, total resources required
- total training days required (and paid), time away from home.

For any of the options, we would urge that major departures in mobilization and training policy be tested in experiments, in which some units maintain the preexisting system while others operate under the new, proposed policy regimen. That permits straightforward comparisons among competing programs and helps to control for other factors that may change over time as the experiment proceeds.

Each of the options we outlined would presumably affect these criteria. For example, the current policy would score lowest on stability of trainees during key training periods; all of the others would rank higher. We suspect also that the current policy imposes more retraining requirements and possibly increased resources for training because of the turnover of personnel after some training events have already taken place. However, the other options may require more time away from home, at least for soldiers who are mobilized. Analyzing these effects quantitatively is beyond the scope of this monograph, but future analyses by DoD or others should consider them to account for the full scope of the effects in making the policy choice.

CHAPTER EIGHT

Conclusions

Instability: Widespread and Enduring

Reserve personnel units are subject to considerable personnel turbulence, in the normal course of events. As we have seen, within a given unit, turnover rates are often in the range of 20 to 30 percent per year, even in peacetime. In wartime, as units approach mobilization and deployment, one might expect the unit to be stabilized to permit efficient and sequential training of the myriad tasks that must be mastered before deployment.

However, our data have shown that *in*stability, rather than stability, is the rule. Across five types of RC units that we studied in detail, covering deployments from 2003 through 2008, RC units experienced substantial instability in their run-up to deployment. Of all the soldiers who actually deployed with those units, 40 to 50 percent were "new arrivals" who had been in the unit less than one year. In spite of that instability—or, in some ways, because of it—those units managed to deploy with 85 to 95 percent of their authorized spaces filled. And they deployed on time; no units missed their latest arrival date specified for debarkation in theater.

This picture of instability is no fluke. We found that it is widespread across all types of deploying units, even those that initially enjoyed high fill rates (e.g., more than 90 percent of authorized positions filled one year before mobilization). Similar levels of instability exist also in active units. In addition, pre-deployment instability affected all grade levels—not just junior enlisted personnel but also NCOs and officers. In fact, officer instability was the highest of all grade groups, owing to the tendency for officers to be transferred out of a deploying unit into another unit—sometimes "cross-leveled" into a unit that deployed even earlier than their source unit. Although we do not have direct measures of leadership performance, it seems evident that this turnover affected the continuity of leadership, and it probably complicated management of units as they prepared for mobilization.

Nevertheless, units did achieve a stable cohort of deployers by the mobilization point. More than 95 percent of soldiers who deployed in these units on D-day were in the unit when it mobilized. So post-mobilization training was conducted in a relatively stable environment, where almost all of those who were to deploy with the unit were able to train together. In contrast, the pre-mobilization period saw a steady buildup of new arrivals joining the unit, particularly during the last six months before mobilization.

Causes and Effects of Instability

What accounts for this instability? In the RC units studied, we identified several factors, primarily personnel losses during the year before deployment and the presence of numerous "non-deployers" in the units at D-day. These two factors prompted a large influx of new people before mobilization. In fact, so many people were moved into the units that, by the deployment date, they were manned at rates of 115 to 125 percent of authorized positions.

A major role was played by personnel losses—soldiers leaving the unit because of moving to another unit or leaving the service entirely. Across the five unit types studied, between 25 and 40 percent of personnel who were assigned to the unit 12 months before mobilization had left the unit during the subsequent year. However, these loss rates may be more benign than the numbers might suggest. First of all, these loss rates appear normal. The fraction of people leaving the service has remained almost constant since the year 2000, and it was no higher during the year before deployment than it was during the preceding year. So losses did not rise appreciably as deployment approached. Second, many of the losses *from the unit* were not losses *from the Army*. Particularly among officers and NCOs, a majority of those leaving the unit had transferred to another unit, and, often, those same soldiers deployed with their new unit. Not infrequently, people being transferred were moving into another unit whose deployment occurred before the source unit, so they were evidently being cross-leveled into a unit with even higher priority.

The other major factor was nondeployers. About 30 percent of soldiers in the RC units at D-day did not deploy. Many different conditions contribute to this picture. Some did not deploy with the unit but then moved to another unit. Some remained at home station and later deployed to the unit in theater, and some were activated and remained at home station, evidently as part of a rear detachment. Some had recent prior activations and so were probably exempted from another deployment for a period of time. Some were new recruits who had not yet completed initial training. And some were not even mobilized.

Among the various groups of losses and nondeployers, it seems likely that, in some cases, they represent an Army accommodation to the service member's personal circumstances or preferences; the Army may have preferred to defer a soldier's deployment or permit a move to another unit rather than lose the person from the Army altogether. Finally, there are many different groups with different conditions that contribute to the overall picture of instability. Most of the groups represent just a small fraction of the problem, and many would be difficult to affect by policy. When we examined a variety of different possible policy interventions, it was clear that, even with multiple policy changes and reasonable degrees of success, a large gap would remain between the unit's targeted deploying strength and the number of its members who would be "stable"—i.e., people who have been in the unit for one year or more upon deployment. We concluded, therefore, that RC units are not likely to reduce instability to the vanishing point. The RC will have to live with a substantial amount of instability in the run-up to mobilization and deployment. And, recall, this is not a problem unique to the reserves; we found essentially the same levels of instability in the AC.[1]

How does this instability affect training as the unit prepares for deployment? The key observation is that many people join the unit during the last six months before mobilization.

---

[1]   Nor is pre-deployment instability a new phenomenon. RAND analysis found similar rates of personnel cross-leveling in deploying active units in the 1990s during the period of stability operations in Bosnia (Polich, Orvis, and Hix, 2000).

Yet, units have been conducting important training events over a longer period of time. When that training is done early, the new arrivals miss key events, and, therefore, the unit must arrange repeat training for them. To examine that process, we plotted the buildup curves of people who eventually deployed to show the inflow of personnel during the last 12 months before deployment, compared with the major training events in unit training plans. In some cases, training on very important topics—such as CTC exercises, combat lifesaver training, urban warfare techniques, and dealing with IEDs—was conducted early enough that 30 to 50 percent of the deployers would have missed them. That pattern was common across all major types of units studied—infantry battalions, MPs, and transportation units.

The implication is that units must conduct repeated training sessions to deal with the many new soldiers who will arrive in the unit during the last few months before mobilization. And, in fact, we saw several unit training plans that included specific "makeup" training precisely for that purpose. That is bound to affect the efficiency of both individual and unit training; the unit's leadership must manage training sessions and events for the new arrivals, expend training support resources to cover them, and perhaps defer follow-on training (e.g., for more-complex tasks or collective training).

Options for Managing Instability: Near Term

A central finding of our analysis is that a large number of different factors contribute to instability. And, each of those factors accounts for only a small fraction of the total instability picture. To reduce instability appreciably, DoD would need varying policies to attack several of the underlying causes. After reviewing the causes that might be amenable to policy change and estimating the plausible levels of results, we concluded that even multiple policy interventions would leave a requirement for many new arrivals in the unit before mobilization. Evidently, personnel instability is an enduring fact of life, and the system will have to cope with it.

How does that affect the policy options that DoD might consider? In the previous chapter, we outlined four alternatives that recognize the likelihood of continuing personnel instability.

- *Stretch training over many months (current policy).* The Army could simply accept existing rates of instability, the need to repeat some training for new arrivals in the unit, the concomitant bill for training resources, and limits on the speed with which the unit can be readied.
- *Cluster training just before mobilization.* If the most-intensive training were compressed into the last five months or so before mobilization and finished up during a short post-mobilization training period, that training would reach 75 to 80 percent of the soldiers who deploy with the unit. The inefficiencies of doing training earlier would be avoided, and most soldiers would be together during key training events. However, such a course also entails some downsides: a greater burden on soldiers, families, and employers concentrated in one time period that may feel like a mobilization. It could also result in lower participation rates if the time demands of training are seen as burdensome.
- *Increase duration of mobilization.* This option would move much of the intensive training into the post-mobilization period, thus relieving the pressure on pre-mobilization and ensuring that soldiers are together for training. An obvious drawback is that it would

require relaxation of limits imposed in recently announced DoD policy, and it would keep soldiers away from their homes and civilian jobs for a longer period of time.

- *Reduce BOG time.* A fourth option would be to concentrate training after mobilization but retain the 12-month timeline on mobilization duration. Consequently, it would reduce BOG time in theater. While gaining the same training advantages as the third option, it would require a faster unit turnover rate in theater and, therefore, more units to cover a given period of operations.

Longer-Term Options

In the short term, the alternatives may be limited to choices like the four options described in the previous section. But what about over the long term—say, three to five years—when policy or circumstances may evolve? Particularly if cyclical deployments continue, the chain of command will surely seek methods of enhancing stability and making training more efficient. Indeed, that impetus would be palpable even in peacetime, with no deployments; all commanders, after all, seek to accomplish more training, more efficiently, and as early as possible.

Framework for Assessing Options

Reflecting on the longer-term possibilities, we asked this question: What kinds of policies are likely to be proposed, and how could DoD assess their possible effects? Figure 8.1 proposes a framework for thinking about the relationship of personnel instability to training, with a view toward assessing the potential effects and resource requirements of various policies.

In this figure, the x-axis represents the level of personnel instability. In the case of any given unit, it might be measured, for example, by the percentage of deploying personnel who have arrived in the unit during the last 12 months.[2] The y-axis represents a measure of training costs, such as the total number of training days spent by personnel in the unit over the preceding year (whether or not those personnel actually deployed). Thus, the more new personnel arrive and the more they require retraining, the greater the repetition of training events—driving up the total number of training days.

The sloping line represents the presumed relationship between instability and training costs. Although we do not have data at present to plot the points on this line, we assume that the greater the level of instability, the more training costs accrue to the unit. Therefore, there is a trade-off between stability and training costs: It will require resource investments to move a unit down the line toward the left, thus increasing stability; but that same movement would reduce training costs, producing offsetting savings. The issues are these: What kinds of policies might be attempted? How much would they reduce instability? How would the resulting stability affect training? And how much less would training cost?

Policy Options for Reducing Instability

At the bottom of the figure, we suggest five possible areas for policy initiatives that might attack instability. Let us briefly discuss each in turn.

---

[2]   Many alternative measures could be considered. For example, to gain finer detail, DoD might measure a fraction of total unit man-days during the year before deployment that were attributable to eventual deployers.

**Figure 8.1
Potential Trade-Offs for Instability Versus Training Cost**

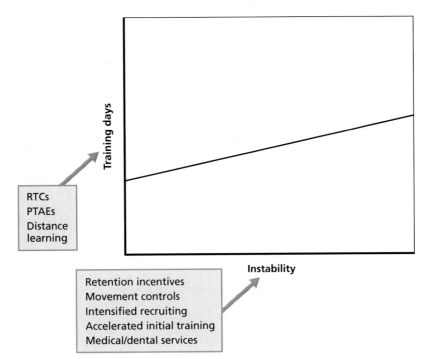

RAND *MG954-8.1*

- *retention incentives:* The service could offer incentives, such as bonuses, to keep soldiers in the unit during the period when the unit is approaching mobilization and deployment. Presumably, the primary cost would be the bonus awards. Such awards could be targeted by unit type, location, or position in the deployment cycle, which would limit costs and increase efficiency. The service would have to experiment with different levels to gauge their effects.

- *movement controls:* The service could impose controls on interunit movements, seeking to discourage personnel from moving out of a unit that is preparing to deploy. However, prohibiting movements by "fiat" might backfire if some soldiers left the Army rather than be required to remain in the same unit. Then retention would suffer, and the Army would incur costs to raise the retention rate back up to its previous level.

- *recruiting:* The service could intensify recruiting effort in units that have many vacancies, like the USAR truck companies we studied. However, the costs might be substantial and would need to be weighed against other alternatives. The service would incur costs not only directly for recruiting (e.g., increasing the number of production recruiters, offering enlistment incentives, boosting advertising) but also for initial training of new nonprior-service recruits. And, since the unit would now have a higher strength, DoD would incur monthly compensation costs for the added personnel who are now in service.

- *accelerated initial training:* Greater attempts could be made to get new recruits to initial training schools promptly. We have found that, on average, new recruits take about 11 months to complete initial entry training. If their training could be scheduled more quickly and training seats were available, the unit would have fewer untrained personnel who cannot deploy. However, this might require more school capacity (e.g., instructors, facilities, equipment) if school seats are already filled.

- *enhanced medical and dental services:* Some of the personnel who do not deploy are limited by medical and dental conditions. The service could invest in more screening, and perhaps in corrective procedures, to reduce the number of medical and dental nondeployables. This is a contentious area: Medical and dental services are costly, recent efforts may already have reached the point of diminishing returns, and many conditions are difficult or expensive to detect before mobilization. However, it is possible that increased screening or treatment could produce downstream dividends, so it might be worthwhile to assess the trade-offs.

Each of these types of initiatives could require substantial investments. If successful, each would move a unit to the left along the line, thus reducing training requirements as depicted on the y-axis. In this figure, we defined the training axis as training man-days, but it could also involve other resources, such as equipment, ranges, instructors, and observer-controllers. Any savings in training resources would tend to offset the costs of the personnel initiatives, but, of course, the magnitude of such savings is uncertain.

Training Policy Options

A different approach, which could be pursued in tandem with personnel initiatives, would be to tackle the efficiency of training directly. The phrases appearing to the left of the y-axis in Figure 8.1 are intended to suggest some possibilities for training initiatives. These might be particularly important if instability persists or is only slightly reduced.

- *centralized training:* If personnel instability remains a problem, it might make sense to conduct more of the unit's pre-mobilization training in centralized facilities, such as RTCs, rather than at home station, and near the mobilization point rather than earlier. Centralized facilities are likely to be more efficient than spreading training across many sites, where each event must be set up and local resources used. Also, professional trainers assigned to centralized facilities would benefit from experience with other units of a similar type.
- *mobile training teams:* If moving the unit to a centralized site proves infeasible, the service could still reap the benefits of professional trainers by creating mobile training units and sending them to conduct special training events or ATs on a rotating schedule. The mobile teams could be configured on a national level and available to rotate across varying sites around the country as local units approach their run-up to deployment. Such teams would probably enjoy economies of scale and be able to draw on their trainers' recent experience. The National Guard already uses a similar strategy with its PTAEs, but they are generally organized at state level.
- *distributed individual training:* Some accounts suggest that a substantial amount of preparation time is devoted to training on skills that are common across unit types, components, and services—such as general military skills, ancillary skills, and theater-specific skills and knowledge. If these skills could be trained using simulation, Web-based training, or distance learning, much individual training might be done by all members of the deploying unit, including soldiers who are physically in another unit but who will join the deploying unit shortly before mobilization. While the initial development of courseware

and infrastructure might be resource-intensive, over the longer term, it might pay off in reduced time devoted to individual training during unit IDT and AT periods.

It is plain that training initiatives of these kinds would impose their own costs. However, arguably, they might improve the efficiency of training enough to produce some savings in trainee time and other resources, such as supplies and equipment. Again, the outcomes are quite uncertain.

Assessing New Programs

Any or all of these things could be tried. In fact, there are perennial suggestions for improving RC personnel and training readiness, and it would be useful to know how well they would work even in peacetime conditions if DoD were not supporting continual RC deployments.

However, as we have argued, no one knows how successful these programs would be or how much they would cost. Conceivably, in the best-case outcome, personnel initiatives might produce a sizable stabilization effect, reduce the need for repeat training, reduce training resource demands, and lead to a better posture at mobilization. Or they might exert only a small effect on stabilization, require sizable investments for incentives and training resources as training is stretched out over time, and produce only minor changes in the unit's posture at mobilization.

Therefore, it would be prudent to test such programs on a small scale before implementing them more widely. For example, the elements of a new program could be tested in a selected set of units or geographic areas. Those "test cells" could then be compared with a control cell that has not received the new programs. DoD has run several such experiments before, mostly in testing effects of recruiting incentives and programs (Buddin and Gresenz, 1994; Polich, Dertouzos, and Press, 1986; Fernandez, 1982). An experimental design of that type would permit outcomes in test and control cells to be tracked and compared over time with a baseline condition to capture time trends and to control for extraneous factors. In the past, such test programs have produced assessments of program effects that have general credibility and provide a firm basis for policymaking.

These ideas, however, are items for a future agenda. In the present, it is important to recognize that personnel instability remains an expected, normal condition of life in military units—both active and reserve. Leadership and policy may adapt to instability or manage it to some degree, but they are not likely to cut it to zero or even to a level at which it can be ignored. So, training policy should recognize the magnitude of personnel turbulence and the many forms in which it occurs, and plan for an environment in which some irreducible amount of instability remains.

Supplementary Data

Percentile Distributions of Fill and Loss Rates

Tables A.1 through A.5 show statistics for each of the five unit types, summarizing distributions of individual unit values for two key parameters:

- *fill rates:* number of assigned personnel as percentage of authorized, at M – 12
- *loss rates:* number of personnel leaving the unit, either "service losses" or "unit moves" during the year between M – 12 and M-day, as a percentage of personnel assigned at M – 12.

For example, Table A.1 shows the following, across all ARNG infantry battalions in the study:

- The median value (50th percentile) for an individual unit was 89 percent. Thus, half of the battalions had values of 89 percent or below, and the remainder had values above 89 percent.
- The 10th percentile was 69 percent, meaning that 10 percent of battalions had fill rates at 69 percent or below.
- The 25th percentile was 79 percent, meaning that 25 percent of battalions had fill rates at 79 percent or below.
- The 75th percentile was 99 percent, meaning that 75 percent of battalions had fill rates at 99 percent or below (i.e., 25 percent had fill rates above 99 percent).
- The 90th percentile was 105 percent, meaning that 90 percent of battalions had fill rates at 105 percent or below (i.e., 10 percent had fill rates above 105 percent).

Table A.1
Percentile Distribution: Fill and Unit Losses, Army National Guard Infantry Battalions

Percentile	Unit Fill: Assigned as Percentage of Authorized (M – 12)	Unit Losses as Percentage of Assigned		
		Service Losses	Unit Moves	Total Losses
10	69	12	5	17
25	79	13	6	19
50 (median)	89	15	8	23
75	99	16	13	29
90	105	19	22	41
Mean	89	15	11	26

Table A.2
Percentile Distribution: Fill and Unit Losses, Army National Guard Military Police Companies

Percentile	Unit Fill: Assigned as Percentage of Authorized (M – 12)	Unit Losses as Percentage of Assigned		
		Service Losses	Unit Moves	Total Losses
10	70	5	5	10
25	82	10	7	17
50 (median)	102	14	14	28
75	113	16	19	35
90	134	21	32	53
Mean	98	14	15	29

Table A.3
Percentile Distribution: Fill and Unit Losses, U.S. Army Reserve Military Police Companies

Percentile	Unit Fill: Assigned as Percentage of Authorized (M – 12)	Unit Losses as Percentage of Assigned		
		Service Losses	Unit Moves	Total Losses
10	83	9	7	16
25	86	17	10	27
50 (median)	109	23	15	38
75	114	29	21	50
90	134	32	29	61
Mean	105	22	17	39

Table A.4
Percentile Distribution: Fill and Unit Losses, Army National Guard Truck Companies

Percentile	Unit Fill: Assigned as Percentage of Authorized (M – 12)	Unit Losses as Percentage of Assigned		
		Service Losses	Unit Moves	Total Losses
10	37	8	3	11
25	57	12	7	19
50 (median)	92	15	13	28
75	104	18	18	36
90	107	23	27	50
Mean	83	15	13	28

Table A.5
Percentile Distribution: Fill and Unit Losses, U.S. Army Reserve Truck Companies

Percentile	Unit Fill: Assigned as Percentage of Authorized (M − 12)	Unit Losses as Percentage of Assigned		
		Service Losses	Unit Moves	Total Losses
10	38	8	5	13
25	44	10	10	20
50 (median)	65	14	16	30
75	96	18	35	53
90	113	26	50	76
Mean	71	16	24	40

Deployer Buildup Curves Before Deployment

Figures A.1 through A.5 exhibit buildup curves, such as those shown in Chapter Six, depicting the tenure of personnel who eventually deployed with the unit, as of the deployment month. For example, Figure A.1 depicts the buildup pattern for infantry battalions. The y-axis values are plotted as a percentage of *deployers* (not assigned or authorized personnel).

Figure A.1 shows that, at 12 months before deployment, about 58 percent of those who eventually deployed were assigned to the unit. By D − 2 months, about 96 percent of eventual deployers were assigned to the unit.

Figures A.2 through A.4 depict the same buildup curves for other types of units.

Figure A.1
Buildup of Deployers, Infantry Battalions

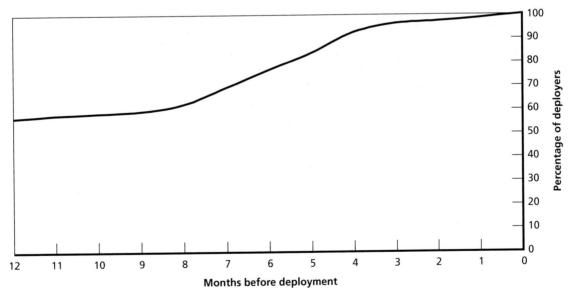

RAND *MG954-A.1*

Figure A.2
Buildup of Deployers, Army National Guard Military Police Companies

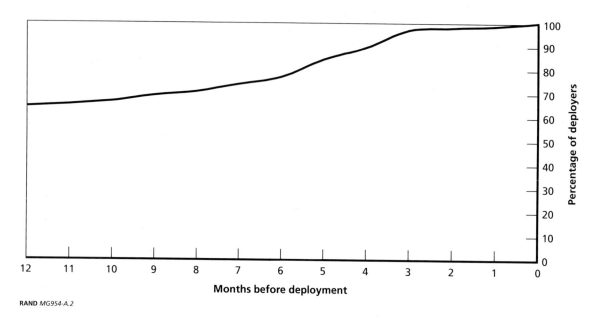

RAND *MG954-A.2*

Figure A.3
Buildup of Deployers, U.S. Army Reserve Military Police Companies

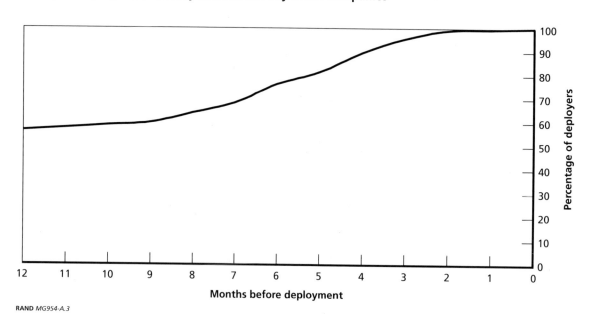

RAND *MG954-A.3*

Figure A.4
Buildup of Deployers, Army National Guard Truck Companies

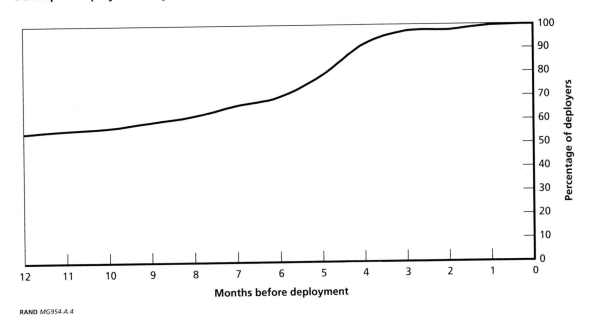

RAND *MG954-A.4*

Figure A.5
Buildup of Deployers, U.S. Army Reserve Truck Companies

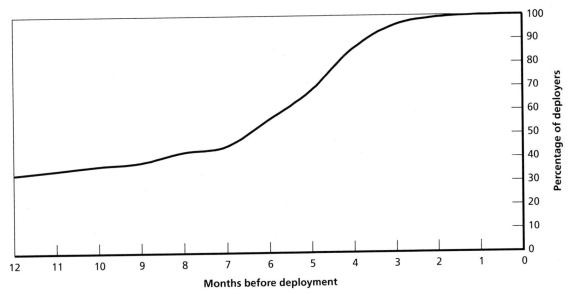

RAND *MG954-A.5*

Bibliography

Brinkerhoff, John R., "A History of Unit Stabilization," *Military Review*, Vol. 84, No. 3, May–June 2004, pp. 27–36.

Buddin, Richard J., and Carole Roan Gresenz, *Assessment of Combined Active/Reserve Recruiting Programs*, Santa Monica, Calif.: RAND Corporation, MR-504-A, 1994. As of March 3, 2010: http://www.rand.org/pubs/monograph_reports/MR504/

Buddin, Richard, and David W. Grissmer, *Skill Qualification and Turbulence in the Army National Guard and Army Reserve*, Santa Monica, Calif.: RAND Corporation, MR-289-RA, 1994. As of April 6, 2010: http://www.rand.org/pubs/monograph_reports/MR289/

DoD—*see* U.S. Department of Defense.

Fernandez, Richard L., *Enlistment Effects and Policy Implications of the Educational Assistance Test Program*, Santa Monica, Calif.: RAND Corporation, R-2935-MRAL, 1982. As of March 3, 2010: http://www.rand.org/pubs/reports/R2935/

Garamone, Jim, "Mullen: Military Leaders Fully Support Afghan Strategy," Armed Forces Information Services, Washington D.C., December 1, 2009. As of March 3, 2010: http://www.jcs.mil/newsarticle.aspx?id=175

Gates, Robert M., Secretary of Defense, Utilization of the Total Force, memorandum, Department of Defense, Washington D.C., January 19, 2007.

Griffith, James, "Further Considerations Concerning the Cohesion-Performance Relation in Military Settings," *Armed Forces and Society*, Vol. 34, No. 1, 2007, pp. 138–147.

Harvey, Francis J., Secretary of the Army, and Peter J. Schoomaker, Army Chief of Staff, *Posture Statement of the United States Army 2005*, presented to the U.S. Congress, Washington D.C., February 6, 2005. As of March 2, 2010: http://handle.dtic.mil/100.2/ADA455326

Hix, William M., Herbert J. Shukiar, Janet M. Hanley, Richard J. Kaplan, Jennifer H. Kawata, Grant N. Marshall, and Peter Stan, *Personnel Turbulence: The Policy Determinants of Permanent Change of Station Moves*, Santa Monica, Calif.: RAND Corporation, MR-938-A, 1998. As of March 3, 2010: http://www.rand.org/pubs/monograph_reports/MR938/

Keesling, Ward, *Effects of Personnel Turbulence on Tank Crew Gunnery Performance: A Review of the Literature*, Alexandria, Va.: U.S. Army Research Institute for the Behavioral and Social Sciences, research note 95-33, April 1995. As of March 2, 2010: http://handle.dtic.mil/100.2/ADA296255

Kirby, Sheila Nataraj, David W. Grissmer, and Priscilla M. Schlegel, *Reassessing Enlisted Reserve Attrition: A Total Force Perspective*, Santa Monica, Calif.: RAND Corporation, N-3521-RA, 1993. As of March 2, 2010: http://www.rand.org/pubs/notes/N3521/

Kolditz, Thomas A., "Research in *In Extremis* Settings: Expanding the Critique of 'Why They Fight,'" *Armed Forces and Society*, Vol. 32, No. 4, 2006, pp. 655–658.

MacCoun, Robert, "What Is Known About Unit Cohesion and Military Performance," in Bernard D. Rostker, Scott A. Harris, James P. Kahan, Erik J. Frinking, C. Neil Fulcher, Lawrence M. Hanser, Paul Koegel, John D. Winkler, Brent A. Boultinghouse, Joanna Heilbrunn, Janet Lever, Robert MacCoun, Peter Tiemeyer, Gail L. Zellman, Sandra H. Berry, Jennifer Hawes-Dawson, Samantha Ravich, Steven L. Schlossman, Timothy Haggarty, Tanjam Jacobson, Ancella Livers, Sherie Mershon, Andrew Cornell, Mark A. Schuster, David E. Kanouse, Raynard Kington, Mark Litwin, Conrad Peter Schmidt, Carl H. Builder, Peter Jacobson, Stephen A. Saltzburg, Roger Allen Brown, William Fedorochko, Bubbles Fisher, John F. Peterson, and James A. Dewar, *Sexual Orientation and U.S. Military Personnel Policy: Options and Assessment*, Santa Monica, Calif.: RAND Corporation, MR-323-OSD, 1993, pp. 283–331. As of March 2, 2010: http://www.rand.org/pubs/monograph_reports/MR323/

MacCoun, Robert, Elizabeth Kier, and Aaron Belkin, "Does Social Cohesion Determine Motivation in Combat? An Old Question with an Old Answer," *Armed Forces and Society*, Vol. 32, No. 4, July 30, 2006, pp. 646–654.

Mullen, Brian, and Carolyn Cooper, "The Relation Between Group Cohesiveness and Performance: An Integration," *Psychological Bulletin*, Vol. 115, No. 2, March 1994, pp. 210–227.

Office of the Assistant Secretary of Defense for Reserve Affairs, *Managing the Reserve Components as an Operational Force*, Washington, D.C., October 2008. As of March 2, 2010: http://ra.defense.gov/documents/RC%20Operational%20Force%20White%20Paper.pdf

Peterson, Jeffrey D., *The Effect of Personnel Stability on Organizational Performance: Do Battalions with Stable Command Groups Achieve Higher Proficiency at the National Training Center?* Santa Monica, Calif.: RAND Corporation, Pardee RAND Graduate School dissertation RGSD-234, 2008. As of March 2, 2010: http://www.rand.org/pubs/rgs_dissertations/RGSD234/

Polich, J. Michael, James N. Dertouzos, and S. James Press, *The Enlistment Bonus Experiment*, Santa Monica, Calif.: RAND Corporation, R-3353-FMP, 1986. As of March 3, 2010: http://www.rand.org/pubs/reports/R3353/

Polich, J. Michael, Bruce R. Orvis, and William M. Hix, *Small Deployments, Big Problems*, Santa Monica, Calif.: RAND Corporation, IP-197, 2000. As of March 3, 2010: http://www.rand.org/pubs/issue_papers/IP197/

Shils, Edward A., and Morris Janowitz, "Cohesion and Disintegration in the Wehrmacht in World War II," *Public Opinion Quarterly*, Vol. 12, No. 2, 1948, pp. 280–315.

Sortor, Ronald E., Thomas F. Lippiatt, J. Michael Polich, and James C. Crowley, *Training Readiness in the Army Reserve Components*, Santa Monica, Calif.: RAND Corporation, MR-474-A, 1994. As of March 2, 2010: http://www.rand.org/pubs/monograph_reports/MR474/

Staw, Barry M., "The Consequences of Turnover," *Journal of Occupational Behavior*, Vol. 1, No. 4, 1980, pp. 253–273.

Stouffer, Samuel A., Edward A. Suchman, Leland C. DeVinney, Shirley A. Star, and Robin M. Williams, eds., *The American Soldier*, Vol. 2: *Combat and Its Aftermath*, Princeton, N.J.: Princeton University Press, 1949.

Towell, Pat, *Forging the Sword: Unit-Manning in the US Army*, Washington, D.C.: Center for Strategic and Budgetary Assessments, September 2004.

U.S. Department of the Army, *Unit Status Reporting: Field Organizations*, Washington, D.C.: Headquarters, Department of the Army, regulation 220-1, December 19, 2006. As of March 3, 2010: http://www.army.mil/usapa/epubs/pdf/r220_1.pdf

U.S. Department of Defense, Managing the Reserve Components as an Operational Force, Washington, D.C., Department of Defense directive 1200.17, October 29, 2008. As of March 2, 2010: http://www.dtic.mil/whs/directives/corres/pdf/120017p.pdf

White, Thomas E., Secretary of the Army, opening remarks prepared for the 2002 Association of the U.S. Army convention, October 2002.

Winkler, John D., "Stability and Cohesion: How Much Is Needed?" in John D. Winkler and Barbara A. Bicksler, eds., *The New Guard and Reserve*, San Ramon, Calif.: Falcon Books, 2008, pp. 29–43.

Wong, Leonard, "Combat Motivation in Today's Soldiers," *Armed Forces and Society*, Vol. 32, No. 4, 2006, pp. 659–663.

Wong, Leonard, Thomas Kolditz, Raymond A. Millen, and Terrence M. Potter, *Why They Fight: Combat Motivation in the Iraq War*, Carlisle, Pa.: Strategic Studies Institute, U.S. Army War College, 2003. As of March 2, 2010:
http://purl.access.gpo.gov/GPO/LPS35591